The
All Blacks
1967

The
All Blacks
1967

Tour of the British Isles and France

DAVID FROST
Rugby Correspondent of
The Guardian

LONDON
WOLFE PUBLISHING LTD

NEW ZEALAND
WHITCOMBE & TOMBS LTD

Made and printed in Great Britain by
The Garden City Press Limited.
Letchworth, Hertfordshire

SBN 72340020 2

Contents

Continued overleaf

The Magnificent Tour

BEFORE THE 1967 All Blacks left New Zealand for their tour of the British Isles and France they were told by Mr Clarrie Gibbons, President of the New Zealand Rugby Union:

'There were times during the 1963–64 tour of Britain when the All Blacks were charged with being over-vigorous and, perhaps, dirty at that ... We charge you to show the thousands who will watch you that we play hard—damned hard—but that we play the ball and not the man.

'Another charge is that we win by playing stodgy Rugby, by using eight forwards and two backs, that we are frightened to run the ball. The style you play will provide the answer to this.'

On both counts the side guided by Saxton, Allen, and Lochore fulfilled its mission. The Meads incident at Murrayfield was regrettable, but it did not sully the reputation of this team as one which played hard—'damned hard' if you like—but was also clean. There is a world of difference between hard Rugby and dirty Rugby. A few people, both in New Zealand and in the British Isles, cannot see the difference. Those who can see it—and they are the ones who matter—know that this side played it clean. The hardness, thank God, was still there. It is the essence of New Zealand's Rugby. Without it as a basis, the second command of Mr Gibbons could not have been fulfilled.

Because New Zealand still has forwards like Meads, Gray, Lochore, Tremain, Hazlett, Muller, and Hopkinson, who by their strength, their toughness, and their skill can get the better of opposing packs, it was possible for Saxton and Allen to put into practice their dream of flowing, open, balanced Rugby. The chief executives of the plan were Kirton, Laidlaw, Davis, and to a lesser extent Going and MacRae. Steel, Birtwistle, and Dick put the finishing touches to it.

Against England these All Blacks for 45 minutes played Rugby of the highest quality I have ever seen. Their match against France B in Toulouse produced the fastest football in my experience. There could never be a more compelling finish to a match and tour than the last few minutes of their wonderful final game against the Barbarians.

These were the great moments. There were also problems and pitfalls. The Meads affair was mishandled by both Saxton and Allen. One or two players could not properly adapt their style to suit the Saxton-Allen conception of Rugby. In this poor Herewini had the saddest of tours, and MacRae was nowhere near as effective as he had been against the 1966 Lions. There were different interpretations of the laws to contend with. Referees in Britain are stricter at the line-out; New Zealand referees are stricter with players lying on the ball. Almost everywhere the All Blacks played, the crowd made a din while kicks at goal were being taken. It would have been fairer to the players concerned and probably more beneficial to the future of Rugby in New Zealand if some of the lesser-known members of the party had been given more games. It was a strenuous tour with a great deal of travelling. If the Irish section of the tour had not been cancelled, the party would have had only one free day in London plus 18 hours at the very end before taking off for home.

Generally, however, it was an immensely successful tour. The final record—played 15; won 14; drawn 1; points for, 294; against, 129—shows that the All Blacks averaged almost 20 points per match in one of the stiffest and most concentrated programmes ever undertaken by a touring side. They scored 54 tries in fifteen games, an average of not much under four tries per match, while their opponents were scoring eleven. With McCormick as their chief kicker—he reached his hundred points in Europe with the last kick of the tour—they converted 30, or more than half, of their 54 tries. By comparison the 1963–64 All Blacks, who had Don Clarke as their No. 1 placekicker, converted 47, or less than half, of their 111 tries (scored in 34 matches).

In the four Tests the 1967 All Blacks scored 13 tries to three by their opponents. They twice had to play Tests on consecutive Saturdays. In five Tests in the 1963–64 season New Zealand scored 38 points. In four Tests in 1967 New Zealand scored 71. The expansive Rugby of Saxton and Allen made the 1967 side much harder to defend against than that of 1963–64.

Whineray's team of 1963–64 has often been adversely criticised for the inflexibility of its methods. But, to put the matter in perspective, it should be remembered that the laws have been changed since the beginning of 1964. It is only now that the changes made by the International Board in January, 1964, keeping threequarter lines further apart, are being fully appreciated. The change made in March, 1967, prohibiting entry into a maul from the 'wrong' side, also seemed tailor-made to facilitate New Zealand's rucking game and so to provide uncluttered, quicker, and more regular possession in the loose.

What made the 1967 All Blacks a great side—some who have been watching Rugby far longer than I have thought they were the greatest team to visit Britain—at least since the First World War—was that, guided by the will of Saxton, they tried at all times to make the fullest possible use of all fifteen members of the side. They did not give up attacking just because they found themselves faced by a defence which at first seemed impenetrable. They had faith that if they went on attacking long enough, a crack would appear. It is remarkable for a side with such a formidable record that they were behind at some stage of each of their last seven games as well as in two other matches. Their perseverance was not the least of their qualities.

The open Rugby the All Blacks played also had the side effect of exhausting their opponents by running them off their feet in the chase. Would this effect have been so marked, and would the All Blacks' record have been so impressive, if they had visited Britain after Christmas when the home players would have been fitter? Could New Zealand make a tour after Christmas in the middle of their own summer? What is the best time of year for a short or medium-length tour to be made from the southern hemisphere to the northern? When the Springboks made their short tour of Ireland and Scotland in April, 1965, they did not win one of their five matches, so lacking in match fitness were they after months of their own summer. This gave the home countries a better chance of victory. Do the home countries want a better chance of victory? Or do they prefer to learn and improve their Rugby by watching and playing against All Black and Springbok sides when these are at their fittest?

There were plenty of lessons for the home countries in the play of the 1967 All Blacks. The New Zealanders arrived at a time when the home countries had tended to be upset by their inferiority in relation to the Rugby of New Zealand and South Africa. They had been trying to improve themselves with coaching, but too often the coaching seemed to be concerned chiefly with theories. Half-digested lessons from the 1963–64 All Blacks about 'second phase' and 'kicking into the box' had been tried out but, being only partly understood, had often led to chaos. Captains had been appalled by the chaos and had withdrawn back into negative football for safety's sake.

The 1967 All Blacks showed that there was no need to be constantly searching for second phase possession: a high proportion of their tries were scored by the backs direct from set pieces. They emphasised that what wins matches is not complicated moves but the ability to do the basic simple things correctly: the lesson here was that coaches in Britain should concentrate on such matters as getting their charges to give and take passes properly. The All Blacks showed that positive attacking Rugby pays. The prime aim should not be to stop opponents from scoring but to try to score more often than your opponents. The way the All Blacks attacked should silence those people in Britain who still believed that coaching necessarily led to defensive-minded, negative football.

The relationship between the All Blacks' manager, their coach, and their captain was a lesson for future Lions tours. There could be no doubt whatsoever, at practices for instance, that Fred Allen was the boss. Yet, though his noisy and emphatic methods drew attention to himself, he did not at all overshadow Brian Lochore. The captain, both from his players and from opponents and public, gained great respect as a man. Lochore was essentially an upright captain who led by his example. He was a very fine No. 8 forward. He also had one game as a lock, and he stood down from only two of the fifteen matches.

Technically the All Blacks gave lessons to both the forwards and the backs of the home countries. They showed the value of wheeling a set scrum so as to wreck your opponents' heel from it. They showed how essential it is to go low into rucks, to stay on your feet, and to keep the eye constantly searching for the ball. They demonstrated to backs that steep alignment must be maintained—there must be no edging forward as the ball is emerging—so that passes will be taken on the burst. They showed that straight running will allow plenty of room for a full-back or wing threequarter to come into the line as an extra man without crowding the outside player towards the touchline.

When they did all these things properly, the All Blacks were a marvellous side to watch. Their formidable collective pace made it sometimes seem as if they had 18 men doing battle with their opponents' 15 as they strove to create a situation in which they really did outnumber their foe, having decoyed some or committed them to tackles.

Of the relative newcomers in the party Strahan, who became Meads's regular partner in the Tests, played a most useful part in the tour. Kirkpatrick, who played in the French Test as a flanker, should have a big future. Williams's pace made him a valuable supporting flanker in the fast open type of game this side played. Of the backs Going proved an entertaining as well as an effective halfback, Cottrell played some convincing games at second five-eighth, and Thorne's promise could not be denied. If these and the other players spread the Saxton-Allen gospel through their domestic Rugby, the influence of the tour could indeed be far-reaching.

In writing the stories of the matches later in the book, I have used New Zealand expressions in referring to New Zealand players and English expressions in referring to players from the home countries. Thus a halfback in New Zealand is a scrum-half in Britain; a wing forward in Britain is a flanker in New Zealand; a stand-off half in Britain is a first five-eighth in New

Zealand. I have set out the teams in the accepted formations of the respective countries, New Zealand teams having three threequarters, two five-eighths, and a halfback, and teams from Britain having four threequarters and two halfbacks. In listing the forwards I have begun with the No. 8, followed him with the four members of the second row, and finished with the front row.

The Unique Conception

THE TOUR was unique in its conception. Normally the longer tours follow a strict rota system with the dates planned many years ahead. But this one was organised at relatively short notice as a direct result of the South African Government's refusal to allow Maoris to be included in the All Black party due, according to the rota, to tour South Africa in 1967.

Referring to his country's apartheid laws, Dr Verwoerd, the then South African Prime Minister, said in September, 1965: 'We expect visitors to behave in accordance with our customs, and I want to add that everybody knows what our customs are.'

The South African Rugby Board, presided over by Dr Danie Craven, did not agree with their government's attitude and did their utmost to get Maoris included in the invitation to the All Blacks. In fact the Board decided unanimously that Maoris should be included. But their efforts were in vain.

The attitude of the New Zealand Government was expressed by Mr Holyoake, the Prime Minister, in February, 1966, when he said: 'Let there be no doubt that the Government regards the principle of full racial equality as basic to New Zealand's way of life. It cannot regard this principle as outweighed or qualified by practices which have domestic application elsewhere in the world.'

Not everyone agreed that this All Black tour in South Africa should be cancelled. Indeed there were Maoris who, with characteristic generosity, said the All Blacks should go to South Africa without Maoris because it was not worth spoiling the fun of the majority for the sake of the three or four Maoris who might get into the party. But on February 24, 1966, South Africa's invitation for an all-white New Zealand team to tour South Africa in 1967 was officially declined by the New Zealand Rugby Union.

This decision set many people in different parts of the world busily trying to think up and arrange alternative tours. The whole matter was discussed at the annual meeting of the International Board which took place in Edinburgh shortly afterwards, on March 17 and 18. This meeting, ironically with Danie Craven in the chair, approved the action taken by New Zealand and 'noted with pleasure that no dispute exists between the unions of South Africa and New Zealand on this point'. The meeting also agreed to a request from New Zealand for permission to negotiate a special tour 'of medium duration' in 1967 in the home countries, France, and Canada.

Meanwhile New Zealand's delegates to the International Board, Tom Morrison and Cec Blazey, had been spending the few days before the meeting dashing about between London, Paris, Dublin, Cardiff, and Edinburgh finding out what the individual unions felt could be organised. The results of all the negotiations were that New Zealand would play matches in England, Wales, France, Scotland, Ireland, and Canada late in 1967; France would advance the date of their scheduled tour of New Zealand from 1970 to 1968. The cancelled All Black visit to South Africa would be replaced for South Africans by a medium-length tour by France, which was to include four Tests.

The details of these tours still had to be worked out, but the International Board probably surprised themselves by the speed at which the outlines were fashioned. It is worth noting here the full and ready co-operation of the French who were still not members of the International Board.

The Four Home Unions' Tours Committee also got down to work so that at a meeting of the Council of the New Zealand Rugby Union in Wellington on August 5, 1966, the Council's firm but warm-hearted chairman, Tom Morrison, was able to present the proposed itinerary for the British Isles section of the All Blacks' visit to Europe as drawn up by the home unions. I attended this meeting and heard the Council accept the itinerary and express their appreciation of the manner in which the home unions had gone out of their way to accommodate New Zealand. The whole affair certainly was a good example of international co-operation in getting things done.

The All Blacks were to arrive in London on October 21, 1967, from Canada and would start with four matches in England. Then they would play two in Wales, including a Test, followed by four in France, two in Scotland, two more in Wales, and finally two in Ireland. There was to be no break in midweek, the matches following one another regularly, Wednesday, Saturday, Wednesday, Saturday, except that the match in France before the French Test would be on a Tuesday. England and Wales would be played on consecutive Saturdays, and so would France and Scotland. There were five Tests to be played within eight weeks. There would be only three matches before the first Test, against England at Twickenham.

In theory there would be no easy games at all. England, for instance, had been divided geographically into three parts, and each region ought to be able to raise a team considerably stronger than the combined county sides traditionally met by touring teams in England. It was a formidable assignment.

The Boss Men

MORE THAN A YEAR before the party for the tour was due to be announced, it was being said that the manager would be Charlie Saxton with Fred Allen as coach. We in Britain remembered Saxton as Major C. K. Saxton, a fine halfback and dashing captain of the New Zealand Army Kiwis in the British Isles in 1945–46. We remembered Allen as Saxton's first five-eighth in the same side. We remembered with gratitude the way those Kiwis had helped to set Rugby in Britain on its feet again at the end of the war. We remembered the unstinting attacking football they had played.

Both Saxton and Allen had started their playing careers in New Zealand before the war. Saxton was born at Kurow, Otago, in 1913, and learnt much of his early Rugby at Otago Boys' High School. He played for Otago in 1935 and 1936 and for South Canterbury in 1937 before becoming an All Black with the New Zealand team in Australia in 1938, when he played in all three Tests. After the war he turned his energy towards administration. After becoming an Otago selector and helping to coach the formidable Otago sides of 1947 to 1950, he became a member of the Council of the New Zealand Rugby Union in 1956 and is still a member.

I got to know Saxton during the Lions' tour in 1966, partly because I wrote in *The Guardian* that the Otago match was one of the two dirtiest matches of the Lions' tour. As chairman of the Otago Rugby Union, he naturally jumped to the defence of Otago in print. In fact I had never said that Otago were the instigators of the stoush. Looking back I feel that Otago played some of the best balanced Rugby—from the point of view of making the utmost use of their points of strength and exposing the Lions' weaknesses—of any side the Lions met.

There was an odd sequel to this incident. Shortly after I got home to England I was asked to talk to the Manchester and District Referees' Society on the subject of New Zealand Rugby and Referees. In the course of my talk, having said that I thought some people in Britain had got an exaggerated impression of the amount of stoush stirred up on the Lions' tour, I pointed out that it might be significant that the two matches I considered the dirtiest—those against Otago and Auckland —had been refereed by the same man. At the end, and after numerous questions, someone walked from the back of the room and said he wanted to introduce himself. With some trepidation I recognised an accent from the other side of the world.

He was, he said, the brother of the man who had refereed those Otago and Auckland matches. Happily his bearing was civil. 'When the All Blacks come to England, do they have to conform to British interpretations of the Laws?' he asked. 'Yes,' I said. 'When the Lions play in New Zealand should they not adapt themselves to New Zealand interpretations?' he said. 'Yes,' I replied. That was all he wanted. We were in basic agreement, and this was the start of one of the most interesting and intelligent post mortems I have had about the Lions' tour. But what a coincidence that this New Zealander should have been on a course in hotel management at Blackpool and was refereeing with the Manchester Society!

Fred Allen was born at Oamaru in 1920, and played for Canterbury in 1939 and 1940. After his war service he captained New Zealand in 1946 and 1947 and was captain of the All Blacks' team in South Africa in 1949. Then he turned to coaching, first with the Grammar Old Boys in Auckland and then with the Auckland provincial side, whom he coached to a record number of defences of the Ranfurly Shield between 1960 and 1963. He was appointed a New Zealand selector in 1964 and Convenor of Selectors in 1966.

I first saw Allen in action as a coach as he was preparing his All Black team for their first Test against the Lions at Dunedin in 1966. It was an impressive performance, especially the concentration on MacRae's short dash on the open side from second five-eighth and his releasing the ball for it to be rucked and switched to the blind side where Williment was to come

2—TAB

up from full-back as reinforcement, running fast and straight.

With the blasé attitude of a critic who has seen a few Tests I expressed a private opinion that this sort of thing always looked grand in training but that it never happened like that in a game. Anyone who saw or read about that Dunedin Test will recall that it *did* happen exactly like that, Williment steaming over for a finely constructed try and New Zealand going on to win by 20 points to three.

Some people in those days thought it a stunt of showmanship that, at the end of every exhausting All Black practice, Allen would make Colin Meads sprint diagonally across the paddock behind all the other players as they let the ball go out in chain passing. Meads had to be outside the wing three-quarter to score in the far corner. Then they would turn round and Meads would have to do it all over again—and probably again as well. Allen's answer came early in the last Test against the Lions. After forward play on the left, the All Blacks sent the ball towards the right corner where Bebb, the Lions' left wing, scrambled it into touch. Someone, too quick for the television cameras, too quick for some of the writers, threw it in and Nathan went over for a try. That someone was Colin Meads.

On that Lions' tour I learned to respect Allen as a man who got things done and got them done in the way he wanted them done. He proved his methods to his players and to his public. New Zealand won the series 4-0.

On this 1967 All Blacks tour, both Saxton and Allen seemed to me to be more or less ideally suited to their jobs as manager and coach. Saxton, whose combination of small size and great authority caused the French to refer to him as Napoleon, always appeared as utterly firm and straight in his dealings with his own players and with anyone else. His sense of humour was never far away, and he was constantly guided by the vision that this side of his would play balanced, attacking Rugby.

Early in the tour Allen told me he believed there were four basic points in coaching which followed one another in natural sequence. The four points were Discipline, Respect, Team Spirit, and Morale. There could be no doubting the discipline he imposed at every training session. Even if his players were merely trotting and sprinting or playing touch Rugby, Allen was emphatically in command. He was the boss: he was the 'Needle'.

Training would begin with a gentle trot round and round the paddock, the pace gradually increasing as the men at the rear took it in turn to sprint to the front of the file. Next there might be a brief period of physical exercises, followed by a longer game of soccer played with a round ball, not with a Rugby ball. After this an oval ball would be produced, and a short game of touch Rugby would be played. All this preliminary work would last something like threequarters of an hour to an hour, after which the party would be split up into the fifteen for the next match and the 'dirt-trackers', those who were not required for the next match. The dirt-trackers would probably move to another paddock to do their training while Allen put the fifteen through their paces for an hour or more of almost ceaseless activity.

The normal procedure would be for the fifteen to rehearse all phases of a game in their proper sequence against no opposition. The fifteen would play as a team with Allen snapping out the orders, calling for a scrum here, a line-out there, a drop-out from the 25. The forwards would churn from a line-out and charge up the paddock, interpassing until the word of command came sharply out of Allen. Instantly the ball would be released. Out it would come along the line of the backs while Allen chanted 'Spin, Spin, Spin, Spin'—forever searching for the perfect rhythm in the passing as he was searching for it in the regrouping of his forwards and backs and the relaunching of attack after attack.

This, it may be said, is roughly what all coaches try to do. Of course they do. But few of them have the authority to impose the discipline he demands. Few of them achieve so much respect. In the case of Allen and these All Blacks his four maxims certainly held good. He demanded Discipline, and they gave him Respect—Team Spirit and Morale were the rewards for everybody.

The All Blacks' Who's Who

WHEN the All Black team for the tour was announced on September 9, 1967, an agency message received in London from Wellington described the omission of Williment, New Zealand's current full-back, as 'one of the greatest bombshells in the history of New Zealand Rugby'. This made strange reading to those of us who had been following the New Zealand season from a distance. Even as far away as Manchester we had heard that Williment had been troubled by a groin injury and that, although he had scored 14 points against Australia in August, he had lost a lot of his mobility, was slow to turn, and was missing tackles. More of a surprise to me was the choice of McCormick as the full-back rather than one of the highly promising young players I had seen playing against the Lions, such as Laurie of Auckland or Henley of Otago. But McCormick was to justify his selection up to the hilt once the tour had started.

The party of 30 included twelve of the fifteen who played in the final Test against the Lions at Auckland in 1966 and twelve of the thirty who had toured the British Isles and France with the 1963–64 All Blacks. There were three Maoris named in the party, Herewini at first five-eighth, Going at half-back, and Nathan on the flank. The party looked a fine balance between experience and youth. The one position where there was a relative shortage of experience was at lock, for Stan Meads had said he could not make himself available for selection. This meant that Colin Meads was the only hardened Test lock, although Strahan had just played against Australia (his first Test), and Jennings had been around a long time.

I was especially pleased that so many of the old hands were going to make the tour because they had so much to teach the players and spectators of the home countries. During the Lions' tour in 1966 I had often wished people from Britain

could see the combined forward technique of, for instance,
Stan and Colin Meads, or of Tremain, Lochore, and Nathan.
I wanted British scrum-halves to watch the masterly passing
technique and football brain of Laidlaw at halfback. Now all
these except Stan Meads were to visit Britain—and I knew the
game in the British Isles would benefit enormously from
watching their methods.

Some of the newcomers, too, were exciting in prospect. I
remembered the non-stop activity of Williams in the Lions'
match against Wellington. I recalled two brilliantly tricky dis-
plays by Going: for North Auckland at Whangarei and for
the Maoris at Auckland. I knew that, with Going and Laidlaw
as the halfbacks, this side could not play dull football. I looked
forward to the attacking running of Thorne who had so suddenly burst into prominence in the trials.

I looked forward, too, to seeing Brian Lochore mature as a
captain. When the Lions arrived in New Zealand in 1966,
Wilson Whineray had retired. It was far from clear who was
to be chosen to replace this great leader in the All Black side.
The candidates included Ken Gray, Colin Meads, Kel Tremain, and Chris Laidlaw as well as Lochore. The choice fell
on Lochore, and he proceeded to win the Test series against
the Lions 4-0. It remained to be seen how he would fare in the
much larger and much more difficult job of leading a party of
30 on a tour on the other side of the world. The 30 were:

WILLIAM FERGUS McCORMICK (Canterbury).

**Full back. Weight 13 st. 1 lb.; height 5 ft. 7½ in.; age 28.
Slaughterman and meat trimmer.**

Played in one Test against the Springboks in 1965. As the
only regular full back in the party he was given plenty of work.
He almost always made mistakes in the first ten minutes of a
match but thereafter was very sound indeed. Had a reputation
of not being a long-range kicker but kicked some long goals
in Britain. Made one wonderful conversion kick from near
touch in wretched conditions in the Welsh Test. Had a re-
markable facility for joining attacks unnoticed by the opposition, especially on the blind side. Very strong physically and
very difficult to stop when in possession.

MALCOLM JOHN DICK (Auckland).

Wing threequarter. Weight 12 st. 13 lb.; height 5 ft. 9 in.; age 26. Company secretary.

Scored 19 tries in 24 games on the All Blacks' tour of the British Isles and France in 1963–64. Since that tour he had been troubled by injuries and played only in three Tests, against South Africa in 1965, against the Lions in 1966, and against Australia in 1967. A neat, balanced runner with a lot of strength in his stride. An unusually reliable handler for a wing threequarter. An intelligent player who scored some good tries, often making them look much simpler than they really were. A fine sense of anticipation and a fair pace. Not a dashing wing but a very effective one.

PHILLIP HIPKINS CLARKE (Marlborough).

Wing threequarter. Weight 13 st. 3 lb.; height 5 ft. 9 in.; age 25. Insurance salesman.

A new All Black who scored three tries in the first of the final trials. A blow on a hamstring suffered in Canada took a long time to mend. A strong runner when fully fit. Brother of Adrian Clarke, first five-eighth, who played for New Zealand in 1958, 1959, and 1960.

ANTONY GORDON STEEL (Canterbury).

Wing threequarter. Weight 12 st.; height 5 ft. 11 in.; age 26. Schoolteacher.

Played in all four Tests against the Lions in 1966 and against Australia in 1967. Former New Zealand 100 yards and 220 yards sprint champion. A player who, like Stuart Watkins of the Lions, often made me want to laugh. Like Watkins, capable of scoring wonderfully exciting tries but also of making appalling elementary mistakes, especially in handling. His dropped passes could often be forgiven because they were caused by trying too hard. A fast direct runner once the ball was safely in his hands. Adept at leaving the blind side and coming into the line on the open side.

WILLIAM MURRAY BIRTWISTLE (Waikato).

Wing threequarter. Weight 11 st. 2 lb.; height 5 ft. 11½ in.; age 28. Sales representative.

Often troubled by injury, he played in four Tests against the 1965 Springboks but—not in a Test against the Lions in 1966. A graceful, long-stepping runner whose balance and ability to weave made him a deceptive opponent. Though not a strong thruster, he was always difficult to stop.

WILLIAM LESLIE DAVIS (Hawkes Bay).

Centre threequarter. Weight 13 st.; height 5 ft. 11½ in.; age 24. Company representative.

Played as a wing threequarter on the 1963–64 All Blacks' tour of the British Isles and France, but not in a Test. His first Test was against Australia in 1967. Fast straight runner and reliable taker of a pass with formidable acceleration. Made some grand tries in Britain and France by drifting inwards, taking a short pass from his second five-eighth on the burst, and linking with his wing. His Hawkes Bay understanding with MacRae was valuable on tour. Varied his game cleverly. Became a key man in the Saxton-Allen flowing open football.

GRAHAME STUART THORNE (Auckland).

Centre threequarter. Weight 13 st. 7 lb.; height 5 ft. 10 in.; age 21. Law student.

A new All Black who became one before playing for his province. Had played in only six first-class matches, including three trials, before being selected for the tour. As a member of Auckland University, made his first appearance in first-class football in the Under-23 trials in August, 1967. A strong centre of great thrust and much promise.

IAN ROBERT MacRAE (Hawkes Bay).

Second five-eighth and Vice Captain. Weight 13 st. 7 lb.; height 6 ft. 1 in.; age 24. Timber company executive.

Played as a centre on the 1963–64 All-Blacks' tour of the British Isles and France without getting into the Test team. Played in all four Tests against the 1966 Lions at second five-eighth—proving himself a very strong runner, ideal for setting up second-phase attacks—and against Australia in 1967. Took a long time to find his true form in Europe in 1967, but his strength was always useful. Lacked something of the fluency required for the Saxton-Allen type of game. An excellent tackler and coverer.

WAYNE DAVID COTTRELL (Canterbury).
Second five-eighth. Weight 12 st. 2 lb.; height 5 ft. 11 in.; age 23.

A new All Black who played a powerful game for Canterbury against the Lions in 1966, showing—among other things—that David Watkins was too small to be used by the Lions as a defender at inside centre in Tests against New Zealand. On tour Cottrell was a most dependable player and showed some of the fluency that MacRae lacked.

GERALD FRANCIS KEMBER (Wellington).
Nominally second five-eighth but really a utility player on tour. Weight 12 st. 12 lb.; height 5 ft. 11½ in.; age 21. Law student.

A new All Black who was a Test reserve against the 1966 Lions. At school he had been a first five-eighth, but on tour his main mission was deputy full back and placekicker to McCormick. He had a wide knowledge for one of his age. One evening in London a Yorkshireman asked those near him to raise their glasses and drink to Wilfred Rhodes. 'What Wilfred Road's this Dave? Is this one of your new motorways?' an All Black quietly asked me. Kember was able to supply the information that Wilfred Rhodes was one of Yorkshire's and England's greatest cricketers and that he had just celebrated his 90th birthday.

EARL WESTON KIRTON (Otago).
First five-eighth. Weight 12 st. 10 lb.; height 5 ft. 9 in.; age 26. Science graduate and dental student.

Toured the British Isles and France with the 1963–64 All Blacks without reaching the Test team. First Test was against England at Twickenham in 1967. Club and representative team-mate of Laidlaw with whom he had a close understanding.

Began the 1967 tour as understudy to Herewini but quickly proved the more suitable first five-eighth for the Saxton-Allen open football. An intelligent prober with a wide variety of attacking gambits. I never saw anyone come into the line a second time more unobtrusively. This was partly because his second five-eighths ran so straight. A very accurate tactical kicker. His combination with Laidlaw in the Welsh Test was superb.

McFARLANE ALEXANDER HEREWINI (Auckland).
First five-eighth. Weight 11 st. 6 lb.; height 5 ft. 6 in.; age 28. Shop proprietor.

First played for New Zealand against Australia in 1962: played in ten Tests between then and the start of the 1967 tour. Toured the British Isles and France with the 1963–64 All Blacks, playing against Ireland and France at first five-eighth and against Scotland at second five-eighth. Played at first five-eighth in all four Tests against the 1966 Lions. Highly skilled at directing play back to his forwards, he found difficulty in Britain and France in 1967 in adapting his methods to the more expansive Rugby demanded by Saxton and Allen. A pity he had not, in previous years, been allowed full freedom to use his natural gifts as a runner. A talented footballer unlucky with injuries and environment.

CHRISTOPHER ROBERT LAIDLAW (Otago).
Halfback. Weight 13 st.; height 5 ft. 9 in.; age 23. Post-graduate student.

Toured the British Isles and France with the 1963–64 All Blacks, winning a place in the last Test of the tour against France. Has been New Zealand's No. 1 halfback ever since, though he missed the Australian Test of 1967 because of injury. Captained New Zealand Colts in Australia in 1964. Capable of making every type of pass to perfection from the long spinner to the gentle push. At his best seemed capable of passing the ball in any direction at any moment. A strong, if not agile, runner and an accurate tactical punter. Has a shrewd football brain and remains cool and collected in the heat of the hottest battles. A master of his craft.

SIDNEY MILTON GOING (North Auckland).

Halfback. Weight 11 st. 8 lb.; height 5 ft. 7 lb.; age 24. Farmer.

His only Test before the tour was against Australia in 1967 when Laidlaw was injured. A player of uncommon agility and persistence, especially in co-operating with his flankers and No. 8 and on the fringes of rucks. His pass was quick, but when he tried to lengthen it he lost accuracy. A clever and neat attacking kicker who always had boundless energy for following kicks. A highly entertaining player, probably third in his position in the world after Laidlaw and Catchpole (Australia).

BRIAN JAMES LOCHORE (Wairarapa).

No. 8 forward and Captain. Weight 15 st. 7 lb.; height 6 ft. 3 in.; age 27. Farmer.

Went on the 1963–64 All Black's tour of the British Isles and France, playing in the Tests against England (because Nathan had broken his jaw) and against Scotland. Took over the captaincy of New Zealand after Wilson Whineray retired at the end of 1965. Captained the All Blacks to victories in all four Tests against the Lions in 1966 and Australia in 1967. Captaincy seemed to improve his play, and both developed a great deal on tour. His aggressive outlook and attacking play matched the intentions of Saxton and Allen, but he was also a wonderfully thoughtful coverer and general defender. An inspiring man as well as a formidable player.

IAN ANDREW KIRKPATRICK (Canterbury).

No. 8 forward. Weight 14 st. 12 lb.; height 6 ft. $2\frac{1}{2}$ in.; age 21. Farmer.

A new All Black who played against the 1966 Lions for Poverty Bay and East Coast at Gisborne. A fast and strong runner who scored some impressive tries when playing on the flank, as he usually did on tour. Forced his way into the Test side against France and played a typically storming game in spite of a broken nose early in the match. A young player who could have a great future.

KELVIN ROBIN TREMAIN (Hawkes Bay).

Flanker. Weight 15 st. 4 lb.; height 6 ft. 2 in.; age 29. Stock agent.

Had already played in 31 Tests—and scored 110 tries in first-class Rugby—when the tour started. Played for New Zealand against the 1959 and 1966 Lions. Toured South Africa and Australia. Was with the 1963–64 All Blacks in the British Isles and France. A strong, bustling flanker with a flair for being in the right place to score tries. As hard and efficient in the close work as he was constructive in the open. At his best a complete footballer. Was troubled on tour by an Achilles tendon and was seldom seen at his best.

WAKA JOSEPH NATHAN (Auckland).

Flanker. Weight 14 st. 6 lb.; height 5 ft. 11 in.; age 27. Sales promotion officer.

First played for New Zealand in 1962 in Australia. Toured the British Isles and France with the 1963–64 All Blacks, playing in the Tests against Wales and France. Broke his jaw in 1963, and again in 1967. Injury kept him out of 1964 Tests against Australia and 1965 Tests against South Africa but he played in all four Tests against the 1966 Lions. Had played in fourteen Tests by the start of the 1967 tour. A strong, eager attacking player difficult to bring down because of the great strength of his legs.

GRAHAM CHARLES WILLIAMS (Wellington).

Flanker. Weight 13 st. 7 lb.; height 6 ft.; age 22. Automotive machinist.

A new All Black who was happy to play on the open side in the English-type open-and-blind system rather than the left-and-right system. An immensely energetic player, he reminds me of John Graham of the 1963–64 All Blacks.

MURRAY CLIFTON WILLS (Taranaki).

Flanker. Weight 14 st.; height 6 ft.; age 25.

A new All Black who alternated between flanker and No. 8 without managing to create the impression that he was a likely Test candidate. The promise he showed in the trials has yet to be fulfilled.

COLIN EARL MEADS (King Country).
Lock. Weight 16 st. 6 lb.; height 6 ft. 4 in.; age 31. Farmer.

At the start of the 1967 tour he had already played in 38 Tests, a record for New Zealand. First Test was in 1957. Toured Australia that year and in 1962. Toured South Africa in 1960 and the British Isles and France in 1963–64. Has played for New Zealand every year since 1957. In spite of his long career he still seemed at the height of his powers and his skill in 1967. Strong scrummager, adroit handler, incomparable rucker. Possessed of an infallible sense of timing in releasing the ball from a line-out or ruck. Powerful yet graceful runner who got a sardonic pleasure from lowering his shoulder into the tackler. A hard, ruthless forager, he occasionally went a bit too far but seldom, in his later years at least, lost touch with a wry sense of amusement and awareness of reality. Unquestionably the most useful all-round forward I have ever seen. A great player who loves his Rugby.

SAMUEL CUNINGHAM STRAHAN (Manawatu).
Lock. Weight 16 st. 3 lb.; height 6 ft. 4½ in.; age 22. Farmer.

His first Test was against Australia in 1967. Developed steadily during the tour and fully justified his selection as Colin Meads's partner in the Tests. He jumped high at No. 5 in the line-out and improved greatly as an all-round forward under the example of Meads. Has still a lot to learn about using all his assets in the rucks.

ARTHUR GRAHN JENNINGS (Bay of Plenty).
Lock. Weight 15 st.; height 6 ft. 4 in.; age 27. Contractor.

A new All Black, part-Fijian by birth. He used his strength well in the scrums and rucks but was not as effective as Strahan at No. 5 in the line-out when partnering Meads.

ALAN EDWARD SMITH (Taranaki).
Lock. Weight 15 st. 7 lb.; height 6 ft. 3 in.; age 24. Farmer.

A new All Black who, like Strahan, improved steadily as the tour progressed. Played especially well against the Scottish Districts when Lochore was his lock partner.

KENNETH FRANCIS GRAY (Wellington).
Prop. Weight 16 st.; height 6 ft. 2 in.; age 29. Farmer.

Had already played 16 times for New Zealand before the start of the tour. First test was on the 1963–64 tour of the British Isles and France. Had a knee cartilage operation a month before the 1967 trials and had to pass a fitness test just before leaving New Zealand. A tight head prop in previous Tests, he played at loose head on this tour. Was kept out of the England Test by a hand injury. Immensely strong in both body and mind. A most effective all-round forward fit to rank with Meads and Lochore.

BRIAN LEO MULLER (Taranaki).
Prop. Weight 17 st.; height 6 ft. 1 in.; age 25. Freezing company worker.

First played for New Zealand against Australia in 1967 when Gray was unfit. His first game for Taranaki was against the 1966 Lions. Rose very quickly to Test football. A strong, solid prop who has not yet developed his full potential.

EDWARD JOHN HAZLETT (Southland).
Prop. Weight 15 st.; height 6 ft. 2 in.; age 28. Farmer.

Captained Southland from lock in their victory in the 1966 Lions' first match in New Zealand. Went on to take Whineray's place at loose head prop in all four Tests against the Lions and also against Australia in 1967. An effective line-out man at 2, 3, or 4. More than useful as an all-round forward.

ALISTER ERNEST HOPKINSON (Canterbury).
Prop. Weight 15 st. 13 lb.; height 6 ft. 2½ in.; age 26. Stock agent.

A new All Black. A knowledgeable, hard-working forward, effective in the rucks. Fought his way to prominence through the trials and proved well worthy of the team.

BRUCE EDWARD McLEOD (Counties).
Hooker. Weight 14 st. 8 lb.; height 5 ft. 11½ in.; age 27. Company representative.

Had played in 11 Tests by the start of the tour. First played for New Zealand against Australia in 1964. Played in all Tests against South Africa in 1965 and the Lions in 1966. Quick breaker from the front of the line-out both in attack and in spoiling. A useful all-round forward as well as a capable hooker.

JOHN MAJOR (Taranaki).
Hooker. Weight 14 st. 4 lb.; height 5 ft. 10 in.; age 27. Farmer.

Toured the British Isles and France with the 1963–64 All Blacks as No. 2 hooker to Denis Young. Was New Zealand's reserve hooker in 1963, 1964, 1965, and 1966. Played in Test against Australia in 1967, but was destined to be No. 2 hooker to McLeod on the 1967 tour. A slow mover but a strong knowledgeable forward. A good man to have on tour.

The selection committee on tour was composed of Saxton, Allen, Lochore, and MacRae. The liaison officers appointed to look after the party were S. R. Couchman (England), Handel C. Rogers (Wales), and A. W. Wilson (Scotland). Ralph Love, member of the Council of the New Zealand Rugby Union and Mayor of Petone, was a semi-detached member of the party.

Organisation v. Amateurism

BETWEEN LEAVING New Zealand on October 10 and arriving at London Airport on October 21, the All Blacks had played two matches in Canada. They had beaten British Columbia 36-3 at Vancouver on October 14 and Eastern Canada 40-3 at Montreal on October 18. The opposition was not strong enough for any attempt to sort out the probable best fifteen from the party of thirty. This was pointed out by Fred Allen on his arrival in London: 'We did not attempt to establish a Test team there,' he said. 'We just mixed everybody up.'

The visit to Canada did, however, produce one serious casualty. Ken Gray, the probable tight head prop for the Tests, broke a bone in his right hand during the match against British Columbia. He was not able to play again until the game against West Wales on November 8 (that is, not until after the English Test and just three days before the Welsh Test). There was therefore, competition for the tight head place between Muller and Hopkinson. Muller, who had deputised for Gray in the jubilee match against Australia—when Gray was recovering from his knee cartilage operation—was given the tight head position in the first match of the tour, against the North of England at Manchester.

The opportunity was also taken of letting Kirton, for the first time, play with Going as his halfback. Kirton had a long-established understanding with Laidlaw, fashioned at university and in games for Otago. Herewini had played numerous Tests with Laidlaw since their first together, against France in Paris on the 1963–64 tour. And Herewini had had opportunities of forming a partnership with Going. But the Going–Kirton link was new.

Otherwise there was nothing especially significant about the chosen fifteen. At that stage it seemed that roughly half this team was likely to play in the first Test. The only change from the originally selected side was that Clarke withdrew with a slightly injured thigh. Steel was therefore called upon for the left wing.

The background to the North's team and its selection is a clear example of the difficulties facing those who clamour for a 'professional approach' in English Rugby. To impose such an approach on a game which has for so long been so 'amateur', so happy-go-lucky in its outlook, will be a much harder task than many people imagine. The English game will not take easily to efficient planning, coaching and organisation.

Since the North as such is never normally called upon to raise a representative side, those responsible for the organisation did some careful planning. It was decided that a match against the All Blacks in October, only the second month of the British season, would leave too little time for all preparations to be squeezed into September and October. Therefore there would be a first North of England trial during the last month of the previous season, in April. Then there would be a match early in September against the England team due to leave soon afterwards for a tour of Canada. After that, early in October, there would be a final trial. The team to meet the All Blacks would be selected after this final trial.

Things started going wrong even before the first trial, which was fixed for Tuesday, April 18. Unfortunately for those organising the trial, the county championship final, involving Durham and Surrey, resulted in a draw. The only date available for the replay was Saturday, April 22, just four days after the date of the trial. Five Durham players withdrew from the trial so as to be fresh for the county final replay. Another five players withdrew for various reasons before the kick-off.

The second part of the programme, the match against England on Wednesday, September 13, went off surprisingly well. It brought a 12-6 victory to the North on Headingley's ground at Leeds. The North's team for this had been announced in the middle of June, so that the players had had plenty of time to prepare themselves. The chief feature of the game was a rousing display by the North's forwards, who upset whatever plans England may have had.

For the final North trial, again fixed for a Tuesday evening, the selectors sensibly chose as their senior side all those who had defeated England—except two, Weston and Pickering, who by now were in Canada with the England team. But things soon started going wrong once more. By the Monday night six players had withdrawn. By the time of the kick-off (5.30 p.m.) there were *twelve* changes from the printed programme, five of them positional. Only seven of the fifteen who had beaten England took the field in the trial, and one of those had to play in a position he had never filled in his life. There was such a shortage of available locks that a club player, who had no pretensions even to county football, found himself pressed into service.

One of the snags of course was that the North side had to be drawn from such a wide area: eight counties, or groups of counties, were involved. The eight were Durham, Yorkshire, Lancashire, Northumberland, Cheshire, Staffordshire, the combined Cumberland and Westmorland, and the combined Nottinghamshire, Lincolnshire and Derbyshire. One sympathised with the selectors. It seemed that the only course for them to take in choosing the side to meet the All Blacks was to go back, as far as was consistent with reasonable form, to the team which had beaten England. After all, some sort of team spirit and understanding should have been built up by that victory.

Sympathy for the selectors vanished, however, when they announced a side which included only three of the eight forwards who had been largely responsible for the defeat of England. Moreover their pack included, at loose head, Coulman who had not played any county championship Rugby for any of the counties from which the North side was supposed to be drawn. Until his selection for the North was announced, his ties had been with the Midland, London, and Home Counties region, who were to form the opposition in the All Blacks' second match. He had played in that region's first trial in April and had played for them, rather than for the North, against England in September. His claim to a place in the North team rested on a letter he had written to Staffordshire saying he wanted to play for them in the coming championship season and not for North Midlands, with whom he had played his championship Rugby every year since 1962.

Coulman's sudden selection for the North seemed unfair to Northern props, and it looked odd when placed alongside the choice of Chapman at stand-off. For Chapman, who had been living in the South of England for several years and travelling up to play for Durham in county matches, had in his turn announced that he would not be coming North to play for them this season. It was not consistent to choose both Coulman, who hoped to play in the North but had not done so, and Chapman, who had played in the North but intended to do so no longer. One other oddity of selection was that John Pallant, who was in England's touring team in Canada and had played for England the previous season both at lock and at No. 8, was left out of the North team.

Nevertheless the side to play the All Blacks included nine England internationals. These were Wrench, Coulman, and Greenwood in the pack and all the backs except Chapman. On paper it was not at all a bad side. There was an obvious weakness in that both the young locks were known as supporters rather than jumpers and catchers for No. 5 at the line-out. There was also no fast English-type open side wing forward specialist—both Greenwood, who had won four caps for England during the previous two seasons, and Barker being regular blind side players. But of the other forwards, Coulman had been England's loose head prop all the previous season and Wrench had won two caps in 1964.

Behind them was Pickering, a better runner than passer, and England's current scrum half. Although Chapman had not had such a distinguished career, the threequarter line included Rudd, who had impressed Whineray's All Blacks with an elusive run and clever try against them for Oxford University in their first match of the 1963–64 tour, and Dee, who had been on the Lions' tour of South Africa in 1962 and was still a quick and alert—though rather small—centre. Jennins, a big strong centre, had won three caps earlier that year, and Ranson had been to New Zealand with England's team on their short tour in 1963. It was a side of considerable experience, even if some of the players were somewhat past their best.

MATCH ONE

v. NORTH OF ENGLAND
AT WHITE CITY, MANCHESTER
WEDNESDAY, OCTOBER 25, 1967

North of England

M. P. Weston (Durham), capt.

E. L. Rudd (Lancashire), J. M. Dee (Durham), C. R. Jennins (Lancashire), J. M. Ranson (Durham)

A. E. Chapman (Durham), R. D. A. Pickering (Yorkshire)

L. J. Rolinson (Staffordshire), J. R. H. Greenwood (Lancashire), A. R. Trickey (Lancashire), S. R. Hipps (Yorkshire), D. E. Barker (Cheshire), M. J. Coulman (North Midlands), J. S. Lansbury (Cheshire), D. F. B. Wrench (Cheshire)

All Blacks

W. F. McCormick

W. M. Birtwistle, W. L. Davis, A. G. Steel

W. D. Cottrell, E. W. Kirton

S. M. Going

B. J. Lochore, capt., G. C. Williams, S. C. Strahan, C. E. Meads, W. J. Nathan, E. J. Hazlett, B. E. McLeod, B. L. Muller

REFEREE: D. J. C. MACMAHON (Scotland)

NORTH OF ENGLAND 3 POINTS

Penalty goal—Chapman

ALL BLACKS 33 POINTS

6 tries—Birtwistle (2), Williams (2), Going, McCormick; 3 conversions—McCormick; 3 penalty goals—McCormick

First Lesson for the English

UNFORTUNATELY the North of England players did not meet as a team until they assembled at noon on the day before the match. They had a team practice that afternoon, but it was too much to expect much teamwork to be achieved in that time. I could not help contrasting this with the thorough and efficient preparation I heard about when I arrived at Invercargill to watch the Lions play the first match of their tour against Southland the year before.

The match itself pointed the same contrast. Southland never allowed the Lions to settle down and went on to beat them 14-8. The All Blacks led only 6-0 at halftime in Manchester, but they played confident attacking Rugby in the second half before winning 33-3.

Yet there were plenty of things to make life difficult for the All Blacks. In the first place there had been a lot of rain shortly before the kick-off, and the ball was awkward to hold. Then there was the universal problem for touring sides of getting used to the local interpretations of the laws, especially those relating to the line-outs. The White City paddock, too, has a reputation for being narrow. The White City is really a greyhound stadium, and the grass in the middle is not used regularly for any sport. In fact, apart from the North's ill-fated final trial, Rugby had probably not been played on it since the Wallabies had visited Manchester the previous season. The in-goal area is very short.

The reason for the choice of the White City is that there are no Rugby Union grounds in the North of England capable of taking a really big crowd. The only exception is Gosforth, in the Newcastle area, which would have been too far from the geographical centre of the North region. Soccer grounds and Rugby League grounds, of which there are many in the Manchester area, are not used nowadays by the Rugby Football Union.

. . . It is as a touring team are running out at the start of their first game that you become conscious of the immense distance they have travelled in search of their Rugby. Until that moment you have looked upon them almost impersonally as just a touring team, even if you have been talking and reminiscing with them. But now, as they loosen their limbs and prepare for the kick-off, you, and probably they, think of their homes and their home towns. You think of them in settings very different from this.

As the great dark frame of Colin Meads moved on to the paddock at Manchester, I caught a glimpse of Wanganui as it was after he and his brother Stan had taken the combined King County-Wanganui team to victory over the Lions by 12-6. It was a good ten minutes before an admiring throng of kids would allow their hero to go in for his shower that evening at Wanganui. And now here he was back in England for his second tour and about to play his ninetieth game for the All Blacks.

I thought of Hazlett and could see him urging his Southland pack to even greater effort against the Lions. And I thought of Going. How marvellously he had controlled and distributed the ball on that dreadfully wet paddock at Whangarei; how cleverly he had run against the Lions for the Maoris. I was glad he had come. But this dog-track in the centre of industrial Manchester seemed very far removed from their own well-loved stamping grounds . . .

A big worry for the All Blacks was probably the frequency with which they gave away penalties, chiefly at the line-outs. The North should indeed have got some early points on the board, for Barker (2), Jennins, and Weston all failed with penalty kicks at goal before the All Blacks scored. In this early period, too, McCormick was far from sure in his handling and punting. The North's supporters probably wished Weston had been at stand-off (instead of full-back) to bombard McCormick with his high up-and-unders. The All Blacks were trying plenty of threequarter movements but, for the most part, these were well held. And the North's defensive worries were eased by a tendency of Steel to let the ball slip from his hands.

It was Steel, however, who was largely responsible for the first points of the tour, scored after 34 minutes. In a movement begun from a line-out on the left, he came into the line on the open side outside Cottrell. Davis was able to put Birtwistle over on the right for a try which McCormick could not convert from far out. Then McCormick kicked a penalty goal. Chapman, the fourth kicker tried by the North, failed with a penalty kick at goal, and halftime arrived with the score at 6-0.

Having witnessed at close quarters the worries of Campbell-Lamerton on the Lions' tour of New Zealand, I knew Lochore would not yet have got anxiety out of his system. The All Blacks had been doing a lot of attacking, but had got only six points. The North could have had fifteen with a reliable place-kicker. Scarcely had the second half begun, however, when the All Blacks hooked the ball at a set scrum on the left near the North's line. They held it, Hazlett hoisted Wrench, and they toyed with the North pack until they thought the moment was ripe to let Going go over for a try on the blind side at the left corner.

This was more like it. Soon Weston started a counter-attack, Ranson released the ball wildly, and Williams ran off for his first try, converted by McCormick. Next came Williams's second try. After a set scrum, Kirton came into the line a second time, Cottrell ran strongly, and Nathan put Williams over. McCormick again converted and then kicked a penalty goal, making it 22-0.

A low, watery sun had now come out behind the All Blacks. The crowd of some 12,000, though disappointed that Jennins had failed with yet another penalty kick at goal for the North, sat back to enjoy the confident attacking football the All Blacks were now playing. Kirton, for ever probing for weaknesses and gaps, pleased the connoisseurs by making a half-opening from which Birtwistle scored his second try. Then Kirton ran left, and Going gave the ball direct from the set scrum to McCormick, who raced over for a try which he converted. Chapman meanwhile had at last given the North three points with a penalty goal, but McCormick kicked another for the All Blacks, making his own personal contribution of points 18.

McCormick had not just scored a high percentage of the points. He had also done a lot of attacking, sometimes adding himself to the line, sometimes coming up unexpectedly on the blind side. Kirton had worked the dummy scissors with Cottrell and had come into the line a second time. We had seen a wing come into the line. These moves of course are as old as the hills. But how refreshing it was to see them carried out so convincingly, and with a wet ball too!

The chief lesson for English Rugby was that—provided backs line back steeply, hold this position, and take their passes at speed—it is perfectly possible for them to score tries direct from set scrums and line-outs. Of the six tries scored in this game, *five* came direct from set scrums or line-outs. The clear message to the English was that they should get back to doing the basic, simple things correctly.

In the evening the All Blacks went back to the Wilmslow club for a reception and supper where they cannot have failed to feel the warmth of the pleasure their performance had brought to local officials and friends of the game. Reg Locker, president of the Rugby Football Union, himself a Lancashire man, was there and made a sincere speech of appreciation. M. R. Steele-Bodger, chairman of the England selectors, was there and so were many well-known Rugby people, including Ossie Glasgow who had been assistant manager of the 1959 Lions in New Zealand.

Wilmslow, twelve miles south of Manchester, had proved in many ways an ideal place to stay and to prepare for the first match. Noticing Laidlaw's absence from training on the Tuesday, I said I hoped he was not seriously hurt. 'Oh, no,' he replied, 'but you can't expect me to go to Fred Allen's sessions every day of the week.' By a strange coincidence, the managing director of the private company owning the hotel at which the All Blacks stayed was the chairman of Salford Rugby League Club who had just signed David Watkins, the former Lions stand-off half, for a fee variously said to be £10,000, £12,000, and £16,000.

A Tragic Beginning . . .

I FELT and wrote in *The Guardian* after the first match that Herewini would have to play very well indeed if he were to keep Kirton out of the side to meet England in the first Test, the fourth match in Britain. For the second match, against the combined Midlands, London, and Home Counties, Herewini was given his chance with Laidlaw as his halfback. They had not played together for five months. Outside them, MacRae, Thorne, Dick, and Clarke, none of whom had played in Manchester, were brought in for the Leicester game. McCormick was retained at full back.

Four of the most experienced forwards in the party, Meads, Nathan, Lochore, and Hazlett, were given a second game. It seemed a wise selection, since the Combined side's pack were all internationals. Hopkinson was offered his chance to dispute the tight head position. This meant a tough, solid pack with the hardened Jennings as partner to Meads at lock and with the three loose forwards, Tremain, Lochore, and Nathan, who had played in all four Tests against the Lions.

This game inevitably will be remembered as the one in which Danny Hearn, playing in the centre for the home side, had to be taken to hospital, paralysed with severe injuries to his spine. It should, therefore, be stated straight away that no New Zealander was in any way to blame for this unfortunate accident.

It occurred in the fourth minute when the All Blacks were endeavouring to bring their threequarters into action. Having no doubt heard how MacRea's strong running played such an important part in the defeats of the Lions in New Zealand the year before, Hearn launched himself with great determination into his first tackle of the game. Hearn, who had won a Blue at Oxford in 1964 and had got six English caps in 1966 and 1967, was well known for his fearless tackling. On this occasion he did not quite time it right: coming at his man slightly from the inside, he bounced off MacRae's left leg or hip. MacRae was not trying to blast a way through at the time: in fact he passed the ball outside him more or less at the same moment as the tackle was begun. The effect of the incident on Hearn was all too painfully clear. Its effect on MacRae was less obvious, but the affair—although he had nothing whatever to feel guilty about—seemed to prey on his mind and to affect his play in subsequent games.

Apart from its tragic aspect, the injury to Hearn greatly heightened the drama of the match. The Counties were forced to take Taylor out of the pack to play in the centre in Hearn's place. As so often happens in such situations, the seven remaining forwards put up a tremendous display. This was a strong pack in any case. In 1965 Horton built himself a reputation of being the most powerful scrummager of all tight head props in the British Isles with the single exception of Ireland's and the Lions' Ray McLoughlin. Judd, also normally a tight head, had been playing for England since 1962, sometimes at loose head, and was England's current captain. Godwin, the hooker, had been on the Lions' tour of South Africa in 1962 but had retired from international football after the 1964 season because he could not afford to miss his work. Owen, like Judd, Godwin, and Rogers, had been to New Zealand on England's short tour of 1963, and he had played 13 times for England. Larter, almost 6 ft. 5 in. tall, was a relative new boy, having played only once for England, against Australia, the previous season. Probably only a knee injury prevented him from winning more caps. Sherriff, an immensely strong No. 8, had won two England caps but had then been dropped in favour of Rollitt, a cleverer handler. Of the wing forwards, Rogers was now only two short of Wavell Wakefield's English record of 31 caps: Taylor, who had achieved a fine understanding with Rogers while they had been playing for the East Midlands, had played five times for England. This pack would probably have offered a brave fight in any circumstances. When reduced to seven they really played their hearts out.

MATCH TWO

v. MIDLANDS, LONDON
AND HOME COUNTIES
AT LEICESTER
SATURDAY, OCTOBER 28, 1967

Combined Counties

R. B. Hiller (Surrey)

J. T. Cox (Surrey), R. D. Hearn (Warwickshire), R. H. Lloyd (Surrey), R. E. Webb (Warwick-shire)

A. J. James (Warwickshire), W. J. Gitings (Warwickshire)

G. A. Sherriff (Middlesex), R. B. Taylor (East Midlands), J. E. Owen (Warwickshire), P. J. Larter (Leicestershire), D. P. Rogers (East Midlands), P. E. Judd (Warwickshire), capt., H. Godwin (Warwickshire), A. L. Horton (Surrey)

All Blacks

W. F. McCormick

M. J. Dick, G. S. Thorne, P. H. Clarke

I. R. MacRae, M. A. Herewini

C. R. Laidlaw

B. J. Lochore, capt., K. R. Tremain, C. E. Meads, A. G. Jennings, W. J. Nathan, E. J. Hazlett, J. Major, E. A. Hopkinson

REFEREE: D. P. D'ARCY (Ireland)

COMBINED COUNTIES 3 POINTS

Try—Lloyd

ALL BLACKS 15 POINTS

Try—Dick; dropped goal—Herewini; 3 penalty goals—McCormick

Chances Missed and Taken

BEHIND THE COUNTIES' pack, Gittings and James were not yet internationals, although James had been on England's tour of Canada. They had played exceptionally well together the previous season against the Wallabies for the Midland Counties, who beat the Australians 17-9 at Coventry. It was James who now put the Counties on to the attack with a high kick towards the left, which McCormick fumbled. Laidlaw came to the rescue and—with a series of wriggles from behind his own line, followed by an astute kick to halfway—took the All Blacks out of immediate danger.

Major had been penalised at the first set scrum of the game. It was after the second set scrum, which the Counties had won against the head, that James had made the kick which had embarrassed McCormick. Now Major was penalised a second time and Larter took an unsuccessful kick at goal. A few minutes later, Meads pushed Owen at a line-out—and Larter failed with another penalty kick at goal. The Counties were getting the early chances they had hoped for but, like the North at Manchester, they were not taking them.

Next it was the All Blacks who started missing chances. They regained the initiative, first by wheeling a scrum towards the open side and taking the ball on at their feet, and then by getting Meads to bore his way through the back of a line-out. But McCormick failed with a penalty kick at goal, Herewini dodged through and passed inside to a forward who slipped. Herewini went through again, MacRae carried on, but a forward dropped his pass at the line. Hereabouts the referee had a word or two with Nathan and Rogers and got them to shake hands after a scuffle at the back of a line-out.

After this incident the Counties followed furiously under another high kick to the left by James, and McCormick was swamped. Then Sherriff made a storming run for the Counties.

Cox went full-out for the corner, and only a grand cover tackle by MacRae kept him out. Lloyd tried a Garryowen, and McCormick had to act quickly. A badly sliced clearance kick by Tremain showed that the All Blacks were under pressure. Halftime arrived with the score still 0-0.

The whistle for halftime was followed by prolonged applause in appreciation for the tremendous battle that had been waged. The dogged courage and the sheer guts of the seven Counties forwards had roused deep feeling in the crowd: an atmosphere had been created such as I have known in England only at a Test. It was good to see so many people in the big stands at the Leicester ground where county matches in mid-week are sometimes played before a mere handful.

During the interval I thought of Arthur Jennings, playing his first match as an All Black. How different was this paddock, not far from the centre of the prosperous industrial city, from that at Rotorua, with its steaming geysers all round and its wooded hills in the background, where he had fought so valiantly against the Lions for Bay of Plenty. I thought too of Mr d'Arcy, the referee from Ireland, who was being very watchful and strict with the line-out play. I felt the All Blacks must now be realising the difficulties the Lions faced the previous year in getting used to New Zealand interpretations at the line-out. The many interruptions for penalties had the effect of breaking up the rhythm of the All Blacks' play.

Soon after the interval the Counties had another chance of taking the lead. This time Owen beat Meads to the ball near the front of a line-out from a throw-in by Dick. Horton relayed the ball to Gittings, whose dropkick did not miss the posts by much. Soon, however, McCormick kicked a good penalty goal and the All Blacks began to look more confident. We saw for the first time Lochore detaching himself from a set scrum, standing out, and getting the ball from Laidlaw in such a position that he had a choice of Herewini or MacRae to pass to. This was a move the All Blacks were to use to deadly effect in later matches.

There was a momentary respite for the Counties when James intercepted, ran and kicked, but Dick got back and covered the danger for the All Blacks. Then the New Zealanders moved inexorably to a lead of 12-0. First McCormick came up to take Laidlaw's pass on the blind side of a set scrum and put Dick over. Next, Herewini dropped a goal after stopping to pick up a bad pass by Laidlaw from a line-out. And then Gittings was caught offside at a set scrum and McCormick kicked his second penalty goal. This, we thought, must be the end of the Counties' resistance. How wrong we were . . . Two minutes later, Larter tapped the ball down from a line-out on the left near halfway. Taylor, a wing forward playing now at outside centre in place of the absent Hearn, slipped inside young Thorne's defence. Cox carried on; and Lloyd supporting him on the inside, just got the ball down over the line with arms outstretched. McCormick's third penalty goal, when Gittings was again caught offside at a set scrum, came as a bit of an anti-climax.

England's selectors showed what they thought of the gallantry of the Counties' forwards by picking all eight en bloc for the Test the following Saturday. But I thought the most apposite comment came from a Frenchman, Denis Lalanne, writing in *L'Equipe*, the French sporting daily. After describing how the seven forwards had battled on against the odds, he went on: 'And when one has seen that, mon Général, when one has seen those fourteen Englishmen rebuild the bridge over the River Kwai undaunted by the best pack in the world, one can be quite sure that the pound sterling is not yet dead!'

From the All Blacks' point of view there were problems. Nathan was found to have broken his jaw, a lot of penalties were given away at the line-outs, and Herewini had not managed to adapt his style to the open Rugby being demanded by Saxton. There was only a week to go before the England Test. By a strange coincidence it was during the week before the Test against England in 1964 that Nathan had broken his jaw, playing in Wales against Llanelli. The problem here was not acute, since Williams had shown energy and pace in the Manchester game.

The question of the line-out was more serious. The referees were insisting on a wider no-man's-land between the two packs than is enforced in New Zealand. They also required the blockers to keep clear of the no-man's-land until later than is normal in New Zealand. It is not at all easy for the habits and spontaneous reactions of several seasons to be suddenly altered —as the Lions found in reverse when they toured New Zealand. Meads's tendency to incur penalties by pushing people out of the way at the front of the line-out was in a different category, and could be put right with a firm word from captain or manager. It has always seemed to be a somewhat pointless extravagance in one whose general play I admire so much—especially when the ball is thrown to some other part of the line-out.

Herewini, who had seemed to be worried by English-type wing forwards on the 1963-64 tour, always appeared in this match to be operating under pressure in spite of fine weather. He often positioned himself so far and flat, in relation to Laidlaw, that a flowing threequarter movement was almost unthinkable. His inside break, his scissors with MacRae, and his kicking were all taking play back towards the forwards in the accepted All Black style of the recent past. In his favour, however, it could be pointed out that the opposing forwards at Leicester had offered a far more spirited resistance than those at Manchester against whom Kirton had played.

Why, it may be asked, was the opposition at Leicester so much more convincing than that at Manchester? One obvious answer is that, at that time, there just was not as much talent available in the North. Of England's party of 22 players who went to Canada, for instance, only three—Weston, Pickering, and Pallant who was overlooked by the North selectors— played their county football in the area covered by the North region. The Midlands, London, and Home Counties contributed 14 to England's party of 22, and the South five.

Incidentally—leaving aside for a moment the regional areas as decided upon for the purpose of providing opposition for these All Blacks—the counties who form the Midland Group of the county championship had by far the biggest representation in the England team which went to Canada. On a county championship basis the Midlands provided 13, the South-west 5, the North 2, and the South-east (roughly the London area) 2. This gives some idea of where the strength of the country's Rugby was to be found.

The regional side which played at Leicester benefited from having a selection committee of only three men, all of whom were former internationals and were in close touch with contemporary Rugby. The three were Tom Berry, who had managed England's short tour of New Zealand in 1963 and who had recently retired from the position of chairman of England's selectors on his appointment as vice-president of the Rugby Football Union; Don White, not so long retired from the field of play and still having much to do with the Northampton club and the East Midlands county side; and Martin Turner who, having converted himself from a wing three-quarter into forward as he lost his speed, was now a top-class referee.

At their trial in April they had organised a match between the Midlands and the combined London and Home Counties, which the Midlands won comfortably 16-5. Their match against England in September did not help their team-building much because England used eight of the region's possible players, but this was a fine game won 19-13 by England. When the regional team to meet the All Blacks was announced, it showed the omission of four players who had been to Canada. These were Savage (wing), Finlan (stand-off), both of whom were to be chosen for England against New Zealand, Richards (hooker) and Broderick (prop).

This region, in short, had the talent. And an efficient organisation to back it.

Tough Opposition

THE MATCH against the South of England at Bristol the following Wednesday, though only three days before the England Test, gave the All Black selectors a chance to see Kirton in action in circumstances more testing than at Manchester.

The South's pack was to include four England internationals and was commanded by Bev Dovey, recognised as one of the most compelling pack-leaders in Britain. The All Blacks themselves, in view of the Test later in the week, would be fielding something less than their best forward combination.

In the pack, Strahan's strength could be more readily evaluated when deprived of the trusty support of Meads, who was due for a rest. Kirkpatrick was given a game on the flank. It looked as if Lochore's powers of leadership would be fully exercised in this relatively inexperienced pack, opposed to an eight drawn exclusively from those tough breeding grounds of West Country forwards, Gloucestershire and Somerset.

Like the other two English regions, the South had begun its preparations with a trial in April at the very end of the previous season. Unlike many trials, this game produced one most welcome piece of evidence. The occasion marked the return to representative Rugby of Don Rutherford, kept out of the game for much of the season by the broken arm he suffered while playing for the Lions against Manawatu and Horowhenua at Palmerston North in July, 1966. In this trial Rutherford kicked 17 points. This was the beginning of a comeback that was to culminate in his selection for England against New Zealand some six months later.

The South had also beaten England 13-8 at Exeter in September. But this was a poor game of countless mistakes in which Rutherford, who contributed a penalty goal and two conversions, was almost the only player to distinguish himself. There seemed to be little doubt that the South's pack could produce a sound performance. And there would be plenty of thrust and pace in the centre, once McFadyean and Frankcom had the ball in their hands.

What the South lacked, and went on searching for until two or three days before the game against the All Blacks, was a reliable stand-off half. A. N. Other filled this position when the eventual team was announced on October 21, the selectors having decided to wait until after Gloucester had played Devon at Bristol on October 28 before naming their stand-off.

Unfortunately for the selectors, a drenched paddock caused the postponement of this county championship match. They then called upon C. R. Tuffley, of Hampshire and the Navy, who was a man of little representative experience and had not played in either the South's April trial or in their game against England. The man who had been generally expected to get the place was T. J. Hopson, who would have played for Gloucestershire if that county match had not been postponed. Hopson had already played against both the 1963–64 All Blacks and the Wallabies of 1966–67.

McFadyean, of course, had been on the Lions' tour and had played in all four Tests against New Zealand, the first on the right wing and the other three at outside centre. Frankcom, a frail-looking but rapid centre, had won four England caps in 1965. Apart from Rutherford's kicking, the locals expected a lot from Starmer-Smith who, although not capped, had recently returned from England's tour of Canada.

But it was on the South's pack that most local hopes were pinned. Dovey had been an unlucky player. He had led the England pack in the only two matches he had played in it (in 1963). In the first instance, England had beaten Wales 13–6 at Cardiff. In the second, a strong Irish team had been held to a score of 0-0 in Dublin. Dovey was promptly dropped. Pullin had hooked against Wales in 1966, and then he too had been dropped for no obvious reason. Watt, at 6 ft. 5 in. an awkward customer at the line-out, and Rollitt, a clever ball player at No. 8, had both been in England's team in their last championship season. They had also both been to Canada with England. Here then was a formidable pack for a touring side to come up against in the midweek before a Test Saturday.

3—TAB

MATCH THREE

v. SOUTH OF ENGLAND
AT BRISTOL
WEDNESDAY, NOVEMBER 1, 1967

South of England

D. *Rutherford (Gloucestershire)*

M. R. *Collins (Gloucestershire), C. W. McFadyean (Somerset), G. P. Frankcom (Somerset), D. H. Prout (Cornwall)*

C. R. *Tuffley (Hampshire), N. C. Starmer-Smith (Oxfordshire)*

D. M. *Rollitt (Gloucestershire), B. Capaldi (Gloucestershire), D. E. J. Watt (Gloucestershire), B. G. Nelmes (Gloucestershire), R. Smith (Gloucestershire), R. V. Grove (Somerset), J. V. Pullin (Gloucestershire), B. A. Dovey (Gloucestershire), capt.*

All Blacks

G. F. *Kember*

W. M. *Birtwistle, W. L. Davis, A. G. Steel*

W. D. *Cottrell, E. W. Kirton*

S. M. *Going*

B. J. *Lochore, capt., G. C. Williams, S. C. Strahan, A. E. Smith, I. A. Kirkpatrick, B. L. Muller, B. E. McLeod, A. E. Hopkinson*

REFEREE: GWYNNE WALTERS (Wales)

SOUTH OF ENGLAND 3 POINTS

Penalty goal—Rutherford

ALL BLACKS 16 POINTS

4 tries—Steel, Kirton, Going, Birtwistle; 2 conversions—Kember

The Captain's Game

As IF the strength of the opposing pack were not enough for the All Blacks to contend with in this midweek match, the weather turned out to be thoroughly unco-operative and the referee was another strict one. A great deal of heavy rain before the kick-off had left the paddock very very muddy. It did not seem likely that anybody, even Kirton and his accomplices, could play open attacking Rugby in such conditions. Yet, after a settling-down period, they had a go and were rewarded with one superb try and another not far behind it in quality.

An early long kick to touch by Rutherford was an indication to the All Blacks that the South were going to be no pushover. Rutherford duly gave the South the lead after some ten minutes' play with a penalty goal from about 45 yards out. This kick, like one before it with which Rutherford had missed the target, was for an offence at a line-out. Gwynne Walters, of Gowerton in Wales, had refereed the All Blacks' match against Newport on the 1963–64 tour which Newport won 3-0, the only defeat those New Zealanders suffered. Now he was watching the line-outs very closely: altogether in this match he was to give 21 penalties against the All Blacks and 19 against the South. Kember was successful with only two out of seven kicks at goal for the All Blacks, but an early attempt nearly brought a try. Watt caught Kember's kick, but had his own attempted clearance kick charged down, and Going all but scored in the corner.

The South, with Dovey getting a lot of fire into his pack and playing a fine game himself, held their lead until midway through the half when the All Blacks scored their best try. Lochore had a lot to do with it. He stood far out of a scrum and, when he got the ball, turned his back on the opposition, masking his intentions. It was a repetition, only more successful this time, of the move he had shown us at Leicester a few days before. Now he dummied to Cottrell, who was running leftwards, and instead passed to Kirton who was going towards the right, and open, side. The South had just managed to check this movement on the right when who should be there but Lochore. The skipper started the ball on its way back to the left. When it got there, having been passed rapidly along the line, the South had nobody available to stop Steel from running over for a try which would have been exceptional even on a dry day. Kember converted, and it was 5-3 to the All Blacks at halftime.

During the interval there was a chance to make a note that the All Black flankers had been playing open and blind rather than left and right. Williams, no stranger to playing on the open side for Wellington, had had a great deal of fast running to do. His style of play was reminding us increasingly of that of John Graham, whom we remembered from the 1963–64 tour. Kirkpatrick, more at home at No. 8, was making a good job of the blind-side position in his first game in Britain. Some people found it ironical that at a time when the England national side had at last come round to the playing of their wing forwards as left and right, the All Blacks should for this match have used the traditional English system of open and blind.

As the game went on, the All Blacks got more and more on top. Pullin won the tight head heels 4-1, but almost the only clean possession from the line-outs came when the All Blacks, sensibly throwing the ball beyond the tall Watt, made use of Lochore at the back of the line. Lochore played a tremendous captain's game, leading his pack from strength to strength in the loose play. It was, I suppose, the first time he had led an All Black pack in which he was the senior player from the point of view of experience. Previously there would always have been Colin Meads or Tremain. Lochore showed true leadership in this match.

Soon after the interval a kick-ahead by the All Blacks had Rutherford running to save with a touchdown just in time, and then an error by him brought the All Blacks their next try. Rutherford miskicked for touch, Kirton grabbed the ball,

Going went with Kirton, and Kirton dived over from Going's return pass. There was another close shave for the South, too, when Lochore broke free and Birtwistle almost scored, but then the South themselves brought off two flowing open movements with Rutherford joining in and Frankcom, McFadyean, and Collins doing their stuff.

Soon, however, Going—as irrepressible as ever—pounced for a try when Starmer-Smith, trying to pass to Rutherford for a clearance from in-goal, failed to control the slippery ball. Finally, in a movement started from a scrum, Kember came up into the line, Davis raced through, and Birtwistle was sent over for an excellent try in the corner. Kember converted from near touch with the last kick of the match. The crowd of some 20,000 had been given as much attractive play as they could conceivably have expected in the conditions. It was a pity they should have descended to shouting 'Off, off, off!' when they disliked some of their visitors' hard play.

Adventurous Omens

KIRTON HAD DULY PROVED himself and was promptly picked for the first five-eighth position for the England Test the following Saturday. The choice of Kirton in preference to Herewini was proof, if anyone needed it, that Saxton meant what he said when he spoke about his All Blacks playing fluent, open Rugby. At Manchester and at Bristol, Kirton had shown that he could launch this type of play. Herewini at Leicester had seemed incapable of cutting himself free from the tighter style of the recent past. It was none the less a brave move on the part of the selectors. An established player of Herewini's experience is not lightly tossed aside.

For Kirton, of course, this meant complete rehabilitation after the unfortunate reputation he acquired as a result of the Newport match on the 1963–64 tour. I was very glad that such a thoroughly capable footballer should at last gain recognition. I had seen him play a highly competent game at second five-eighth against Ulster in Belfast in 1964. He had also played finely controlled attacking football for Otago against the 1966 Lions and, incidentally, in the curtain-raiser to the first Test in Dunedin.

There were no big surprises in this All Black team to meet England. Birtwistle was preferred to Steel for the left wing, presumably because Steel's handling had been uncertain. Williams took the injured Nathan's place on the flank, and Muller was the tight head. The tall Strahan was preferred to the tough Jennings as Meads's partner at lock—a choice which suggested that the All Blacks wanted to get initial possession at the line-out for attacking purposes, rather than to wrench the ball from the grasp of opponents. It seemed that the choice of Strahan, taken together with the choice of Kirton, was a good omen for an adventurous game at Twickenham.

Since New Zealand last played England, in January, 1964,

England had not been having much success. In that period they had won four games, drawn three and lost ten. At the beginning of the 1966–67 season they took the unorthodox step of calling out of retirement Richard Sharp, a beautiful stand-off half at his best, and asking him to captain the side. This did not save them from being beaten 23-11 by Australia in their first match of the season. For their second match, against Ireland in Dublin, the selectors (M. R. Steele-Bodger, D. B. Vaughan, A. E. Agar, E. Evans, J. F. Butterfield, and R. E. G. Jeeps) made many changes, including a new scrum-half, Pickering, a new stand-off, Finlan, and five different forwards. Perhaps more important was the appointment of a new captain, Judd.

In both 1965 and 1967 Phil Judd had captained the senior side in England's final trial, but had not then been nominated captain of England. He had had a lot of experience as captain of the Coventry club and of the Warwickshire county side. Now was his chance. His influence was seen chiefly in the way the England forwards buckled down to their task and kept on going no matter what went wrong. He also seemed to instil a feeling that risks were worth taking. England were rather lucky to beat Ireland with a last-minute try but, although they lost 12-16 to France (the eventual champions), their new adventurous style brought about the defeat of Scotland by the remarkable score of 27-14. The pitfalls of this risky Rugby were shown when England went down to Cardiff on a balmy day in April and lost their last match of the season 21-34. But England had now become an entertaining side to watch.

Meanwhile the zeal for coaching had spread to the England selectors themselves. They began the practice of getting the 30-odd players assembled for an England trial to stay on at the venue for what became known as 'teach-ins' on the Sundays. It was hoped that these would lead to a common purpose in England's players.

A further novelty, inspired by Steele-Bodger and his committee, was the series of three regional matches played by England against the regions in the September before the All Blacks were due to arrive. It was generally reckoned that these matches would serve three useful purposes. They would enable the England players to get some match practice before their imminent tour of Canada. They would also allow the regions to produce something rather better than utterly scratch sides to face the All Blacks. And they would also provide the possibility that England, after the three matches against the regions and then a five-match tour of Canada, would have a fifteen showing a degree of purposeful teamwork rarely achieved by one of the home countries.

From the point of view of results, the tour of Canada—with five matches between September 23 and October 7—was a success. England scored 164 points, did not have their line crossed, and had only nine points scored against them. They beat Alberta 22-3 at Calgary, British Columbia 27-0 at Victoria, Canada 29-0 at Vancouver, Ontario 33-3 at Toronto, and Eastern Canada 53-3 at Ottawa. Canadian Rugby, of course, is not yet strong. But this tour should have enabled England to forge a team of more than usual competence.

Yet, when the England team to meet New Zealand was announced, it included seven players who were not among the 22 (picked early in May) who went to Canada. Only four of the chosen fifteen had not played against the All Blacks at Leicester. The four were three 1966 Lions—Rutherford, Savage, and McFadyean—together with Finlan, who had been England's stand-off in their last four matches of the previous season but had, like Savage, been passed over by the regional selectors for the Leicester match.

Judd, Godwin, and Rogers would be playing against New Zealand for the fourth time. They played in both the Tests on England's short tour in 1963 as well as at Twickenham in 1964. Owen played in one of the 1963 tour Tests and in the Twickenham game. He, incidentally, played in the Leicester regional match only because John Barton, a colleague of Owen both for Coventry and for Warwickshire, had water on the knee. Barton had played three games for England the previous season.

Behind the scrum, Gittings was winning his first cap at the age of 28. He gained preference over the North's Pickering presumably because, although not such a naturally gifted player, he had shown himself at Leicester capable of getting through a lot of tough, almost Jeeps-like work at close quarters. The only other new cap in the fifteen was Lloyd, a 24-year-old Harlequin who had scored against the All Blacks at Leicester and was destined to score three more tries at Twickenham, thus becoming the only Englishman to score a try against the All Blacks on this tour. Apart from Lloyd, standing in for the unfortunate Hearn, the threequarters were those who had represented England in their last two matches of the previous season.

Saxton had told us that New Zealand would play free attacking Rugby. We had reason to believe England would too. Their three matches at Twickenham the previous season, against Australia, France, and Scotland, had produced an aggregate of 103 points, of which England had scored 50. These had been followed by that extraordinary game against Wales at Cardiff which had produced 55 points. It looked as if the Queen and Prince Philip were to be given plenty of entertainment by both England and New Zealand. England's chances of winning, we felt, were slight and depended very largely on whether their forwards could rouse themselves twice in so short a space of time to the great heights of endeavour they had displayed at Leicester the week before.

This they could not quite do. The same inspiration just was not there. But they played doggedly none the less, as they surely always will with Judd as captain. New Zealand were made to play superbly in running into a lead of 18-0 shortly before the interval and one of 23-5 soon afterwards. This almost unassailable lead was one reason why the match was not wholly satisfying as a spectacle for its full 80 minutes. Almost inevitably it rather went off the boil in the second half. The judgment of MacRae, too, was a little awry at times, and some of the palming of Strahan at the line-outs produced such erratic possession that even Meads and Lochore could not always clear up the mess. But these were minor blemishes on a grand display by the All Blacks, and they took none of the pleasure and excitement away from an unforgettable first 45 minutes.

MATCH FOUR

v. ENGLAND
AT TWICKENHAM
SATURDAY, NOVEMBER 4, 1967

England

D. Rutherford (Gloucester)

K. F. Savage (Northampton), C. W. McFadyean (Moseley), R. H. Lloyd (Harlequins), R. E. Webb (Coventry)

J. F. Finlan (Moseley), W. J. Gittings (Coventry)

G. A. Sherriff (Saracens), R. B. Taylor (Northampton), J. E. Owen (Coventry), P. J. Larter (Northampton), D. P. Rogers (Bedford), P. E. Judd (Coventry), capt., H. Godwin (Coventry), A. L. Horton (Blackheath)

New Zealand

W. F. McCormick

M. J. Dick, W. L. Davis, W. M. Birtwistle

I. R. MacRae, E. W. Kirton

C. R. Laidlaw

B. J. Lochore, capt., K. R. Tremain, S. C. Strahan, C. E. Meads, G. C. Williams, E. J. Hazlett, B. E. McLeod, B. L. Muller

REFEREE: D. J. C. MACMAHON (Scotland)

ENGLAND 11 POINTS

2 tries—Lloyd (2); conversion—Rutherford; penalty goal—Larter

NEW ZEALAND 23 POINTS

5 tries—Kirton (2), Birtwistle, Laidlaw, Dick; 4 conversions—McCormick

A Great Day

A LOT OF RAIN had fallen, and though this stopped in time for the start of the match, it was a dull and grey day, and Twickenham's grass remained heavy with water. A red carpet was rolled out for the Queen to inspect the two teams, but Twickenham's huge tall stands looked more gaunt than ever as the anthem was played and sung. New Zealand wheeled the first scrum to the open side and took the ball on at their feet. Rutherford fielded a kick in his own 25, sold a dummy, ran, and gave the ball to his centres. New Zealand took a tapped penalty and ran from inside their own half. This was what we wanted. We knew we were in for something good.

We did not have long to wait for the first New Zealand try. After seven minutes' play the ball went astray from a wild pass by Gittings from a line-out on New Zealand's left. Meads and company chased after it, Davis made a run on the left of the ruck near England's posts, Kirton scored, and McCormick converted from about halfway out (5-0). There was a brief moment of anxiety for New Zealand when a high kick by McFadyean caused McCormick to fumble, as he usually did in the first quarter of an hour of a match, but then Rogers got offside at a set scrum and McCormick took a long penalty kick at goal. He missed with this kick, and when he next came up into the line with his backs, England's marking, tackling, and spoiling were sound and quick, and the move lost New Zealand a lot of ground.

To their great credit, New Zealand went on attacking in this way, and even got McCormick to make a dummy entry into the line while they by-passed him with a long pass to the man outside. As a variation Kirton lofted a towering Garryowen, but England cleared after a set scrum had been called. England tried to attack by getting Gittings to run from a set scrum and pass to Rogers, breaking quickly. But Rogers dropped the ball. The play was already going New Zealand's way and soon, after 27 minutes, Williams used his formidable acceleration to get clear of some loose play. He kicked ahead, and in the pursuit Birtwistle scored a try which McCormick converted, this time from near touch (10-0).

England were being kept under almost constant pressure now—as Williams made a rapid run from a set scrum, a cross-kick by Kirton hit a goalpost, and Kirton sent across a perfectly angled diagonal kick. It was just after this that Laidlaw, wily as ever if not quite at his best, dived literally under the noses of the England pack to touch down a ball hooked but not yet heeled by England at a set scrum on their line (13-0). Play had hardly been restarted when the All Blacks, eight minutes before halftime, checked a heel from a set scrum on the left just long enough for Lochore to detach himself towards the open side. There he took Laidlaw's pass and dragged the England defence towards him before releasing the ball towards the blind side, where Kirton just managed to get over in the corner. It was a wonderfully clever try deserving McCormick's superb conversion from near touch (18-0).

For the last few minutes of this first half we saw England fighting back defiantly. A high kick by Gittings had McCormick swamped by England's desperate following-up, and New Zealand were penalised. Rutherford, however, missed with the kick from just to the left of the posts, and it looked as if England would arrive at halftime without a score. No sooner had this been thought than the England backs had one of their two moments of glory. After a set scrum on the right, near halfway in the last minute of the half, Savage left the blind side and raced into the line on the open side. A breach was made, McFadyean carried on, Lloyd scored on the left, and this time Rutherford made no mistake with his kick (18-5). Fred Allen generously said afterwards that he thought this was the best try of the match.

After halftime New Zealand returned to the attack, and MacRae made a searing break outside McFadyean. Then, three minutes after the interval, came a really brilliantly executed backs' try: the two Hawkes Bay men, MacRae and Davis, brought off a perfect 'close', as we call it in the North of England. After a line-out on the left near halfway, Davis floated in to take a short pass from MacRae, floated out again, straightened, and gave Dick the scoring pass at the last defender. McCormick converted off a post, and there it was— 23-5 and the second half barely started.

England sent the subsequent kick-off the 'wrong' way straight to Savage. He ran hard up the right touchline before passing to Taylor, who very nearly got over for what would have been a most unusual try. England from now on were to have rather the better of the game territorially, but their basic technique in handling was not sound enough for coping with such a wet ball. This fault ought to have cost them another try when Webb came into the England line from the blind side and dropped the ball. MacRae ran off with it with two men outside him, but he tried to sell a dummy and the chance was gone. The All Blacks missed another chance when McCormick failed with a fairly simple penalty kick at goal. Then Larter failed with a difficult penalty kick at goal for England. This penalty kick of Larter's was given for an offence by the All Blacks at a line-out, but generally they offended much less here than in their previous games. It was not clear to what extent this was due to their own efforts at adapting their drills or to less strict refereeing. It was noticeable that in this match Mr MacMahon watched the line-outs chiefly from the back whereas at Manchester he had watched them chiefly from the front.

In the last twenty minutes England belatedly started using a mini line-out. The first time they tried it Gittings ran close to the touchline and passed inside to his forwards, and the second time the ball was tapped down to Sherriff who used his strength to barge his way through. Finlan had a drop at goal, Gittings and Finlan worked a dummy scissors and Gittings passed direct to one of his centres, and then Larter kicked a penalty goal. By this time the game had really gone off the boil, but in the last move of the day Finlan crosskicked from the right, Dick was swamped by England, and Lloyd ran over for his second try of the match, his third in two games against the All Blacks. The final score, 23-11, was the same as that of the England-Australia match the previous season. It meant that England's last four games at Twickenham had brought the crowd the impressive aggregate of 137 points.

The message from New Zealand was that the surest way of winning at Rugby football is to do the basic things more correctly and more efficiently than your opponents. All eight New Zealand forwards had pushed their weight at the scrums. They had brought off one or two masterly wheels. They had torn into the rucks with not an instant's hesitation. They had backed up tirelessly. They and the backs had kept their eyes steadfastly fixed on the ball. Passes were accurately given and watchfully taken. So sound was the basic technique that the All Blacks scored five tries with a ball that the English generally found unmanageably slippery. Two of these New Zealand tries could not have been more perfectly executed had the ball and the ground been dry. To an England in which theorising and the coaching of fancy moves had become something like an obsession, the message was 'back to square one'. In their four matches in England, the All Blacks had scored 89 points against 20. They had scored 16 tries against three.

That night London seemed full of New Zealanders. Something like four hundred Kiwi supporters had recently arrived, having paid about £700 to watch the tour—they were to turn up loyally even in distant parts of France—and there were thought to be about 2,000 resident in London. There was Bob Scott, there was Jack Finlay, there was Roger Urbahn. I even bumped into Geoff Bailey. Ralph Love was there of course, and Wally Birdsall was there. The Rugby Football Union gave a dinner at the London Hilton Hotel at which well over 300 people were present. It was a great day for Charlie Saxton, for Fred Allen, and for Brian Lochore.

The Welsh Make Ready

Now IT WAS time for the first of the two visits to Wales, where the new emphasis on coaching was expected to funnel Welsh fervour towards even more purposeful activity than had been faced by earlier visitors. The first match in Wales, on the Wednesday before the Welsh Test, was to be at Swansea against a combined side representing West Wales.

The most important item in the All Blacks' selecting for this match was that the hand Ken Gray injured in Vancouver was now sufficiently mended for him to take the field for his first game of the tour in Britain. This injury had not of course prevented him from keeping the rest of his body fit, so that there was a chance he might find a place in the Test team against Wales the following Saturday. Wills, on the flank, was also to have his first game in Britain.

Lochore at last decided to have a rest, which meant that Kirkpatrick could have a game at No. 8 and that a captain for the day had to be appointed. MacRae, the official vice-captain, was also resting in view of the Saturday Test, so the captaincy was given to Meads who would be playing his ninety-third game in an All Black jersey. Of the fifteen who had played against England, only Meads and Tremain were included in the team for the match against West Wales.

England, with their Sunday teach-ins for trials players the previous season, had made a step forward in their coaching. Wales went a couple of steps further at least. First Ray Williams, who had done a lot of valuable work with the Rugby Football Union's coaching panel in producing the R.F.U.'s ambitious coaching manual, was appointed to be their professional coach-organiser—the first of his kind in any of the home countries. Then, early in the September before the All Blacks arrived, the Welsh Rugby Union sanctioned a recommendation from their selection committee that a squad of players should meet regularly to be coached as a national team. They agreed that the man to do this coaching of the national squad was David Nash, who had recently made Welsh Rugby history by being the first man appointed to the national selection committee from outside the Welsh Rugby Union. Nash, who had won six Welsh caps in 1961 and 1962 and had been on the Lions' tour of South Africa in 1962, was still in his twenties.

At the same time, coaches were appointed to look after the squads from which were to be chosen the teams to represent West Wales and East Wales against the All Blacks. The coach of the West squad was to be Caerwyn James, a former Llanelli and Wales stand-off half, who had played against Australia and France in 1958. The East's coach was named as Dai Hayward, a former Cardiff wing forward who had played six times for Wales in 1963 and 1964, including the 1964 match against New Zealand. The Welsh R.U. also decided that the captain of Wales would be announced before the national team was chosen and that he and the national coach would sit in on the final selection committee.

Lest anyone should imagine that Monmouthshire, the other Welsh side due to meet the All Backs, were left out of these arrangements, it should be pointed out that it was they, in fact, who gave the lead. They had announced during the summer that their coach would be David Harries, the Newbridge club coach, and they also announced the names of more than twenty players who would come under his coaching in preparation for the match against the All Blacks at Newport on December 6. Such a thorough organisation had never been known anywhere in the British Isles before.

In the West Wales preparation, there was another V.I.P., besides the coach, who mattered a great deal. This was Clive Rowlands, a former Welsh captain and scrum-half, who had in fact captained Wales against the 1963–64 All Blacks. In those days his club had been Pontypool, in the East, but he had since then switched his loyalties to Swansea and had taken over the captaincy there.

Rowlands was a man of strong personality who had had the distinction of captaining his country on his first Test appearance, in the 1962–63 season. He was always a controversial figure in Test Rugby because of his emphasis on kicking. It was said that his pass was not long enough or quick enough to give David Watkins, his Test partner, a chance to show his paces as a runner. He was criticised for being a dictator and an individualist. He was blamed repeatedly for imposing dull tactics.

It often seemed to me that those who judged Rowlands most harshly in his Test days were those who had seen him play only on television. I suppose when we switch on television we expect to be entertained in some spectacular fashion. If there is not much spectacle or movement, we are disappointed. Certainly there was seldom anything very spectacular about Wales's play under Rowlands. But, as captain of the Welsh Rugby team, he was not there to be spectacular. He was there to try to win matches. And in his last season, in 1965, Wales beat all three of England, Scotland, and Ireland and so won the Triple Crown for the first time for thirteen years.

Rowlands had achieved his notoriety in his second match, against Scotland at Murrayfield in 1963, when his incessant kicking had exasperated both television viewers and Scotland, but Wales had won by a dropped goal and a penalty goal to nothing. Somehow you were either all for Rowlands or dead against him. His style always fascinated me for its singlemindedness and I never failed to enjoy watching Wales play under him. What he was really doing was making use of what assets his Welsh side had and at the same time hiding its deficiencies. He had a big and solid pack which was highly efficient at the set scrums and, especially, at the line-out. By his kicking, as often as not parallel to the touchline, he was forcing his opponents to scramble the ball into touch, thereby gaining another throw-in for Wales. He was also hoping that a mistake in handling would present a try for his blind-side wing threequarter.

At the same time Rowlands was successfully hiding the fact that this big pack of his was extremely slow if forced to move about the field. France, of course, were the dangerous team for Rowlands because of their ability to impose a fast game. It is no mere coincidence that the three games his Welsh side played against France ended in two victories for France and a draw. In the last of the three, France actually scored 19 points in the first half before winning 22-13. Rowlands inevitably was blamed for this defeat by those who had forgotten how skilfully he had until then hidden Wales's weaknesses. He was accused of directing negative Rugby. But to make the best of your side's limited assets is not negative Rugby.

Now Rowlands was to captain West Wales against the All Blacks in what was expected to be his last big representative match. He and Caerwyn James schemed carefully and spent a lot of time getting any feeling of inferiority out of their men. Rowlands was to use his kicking parallel to the touchline to force the All Blacks to put the ball into touch, thus giving the Welsh the throw-in, and the Welsh would employ a mini line-out, consisting of sometimes three, sometimes four men. They would vary this with a long throw right over the back of the line. They would try by such means to upset the pattern of the All Blacks' play.

The West had few other players of wide reputation except Delme Thomas, who had played in two Tests for the Lions against New Zealand in 1966 and whose line-out skill was to mean much to the West in this match. Of the rest Morris, the blind-side wing forward, had played twice for Wales the previous season as a No. 8, and Byron Gale was a brother of Norman Gale, the current Wales captain.

MATCH FIVE

v. WEST WALES
AT SWANSEA
WEDNESDAY, NOVEMBER 8, 1967

West Wales

D. Rees (Swansea)

H. Rees (Neath), J. Davies (Swansea), C. Jones (Aberavon), H. Williams (Neath)

J. K. Evans (Neath), D. C. T. Rowlands (Swansea), capt.

R. Wanbon (Aberavon), M. Evans (Swansea), W. D. Thomas (Llanelli), B. Davies (Neath), D. Morris (Neath), R. B. Gale (Llanelli), R. Thomas (Swansea), W. Williams (Neath)

All Blacks

G. F. Kember

P. H. Clarke, G. S. Thorne, A. G. Steel

W. D. Cottrell, M. A. Herewini

S. M. Going

I. A. Kirkpatrick, K. R. Tremain, A. G. Jennings, C. E. Meads, capt., M. C. Wills, K. F. Gray, J. Major, A. E. Hopkinson

REFEREE: M. H. TITCOMB (England)

WEST WALES 14 POINTS

try—H. Williams; 3 penalty goals—D. Rees; conversion—D. Rees

ALL BLACKS 21 POINTS

4 tries—Thorne (2), Meads, Going; 3 conversions—Kember; penalty goal—Kember

A Fight all the Way

ONE REASON why West Wales could get together for the regular practice which was denied, for instance, to the North of England, was that all the leading clubs of West Wales are grouped in one small area. Swansea, Neath, Llanelli, and Aberavon are within a stone's throw as compared with the distance separating the north of Northumberland, say, from the south of Staffordshire. Indeed, all the big clubs of Welsh Rugby are to be found along that narrow belt in the south of the country. This togetherness means that everybody seems to know everybody else in Welsh Rugby, and this in turn accounts in part for the compelling intimacy of a Welsh Rugby crowd.

On this occasion the crowd of some 35,000 soon had a local hero to take to their hearts. This was Doug Rees, the Swansea full-back, who was in his first season of first-class Rugby. After only three minutes' play he banged over a penalty goal from 40 yards. Ten minutes later another penalty kick of his, this time from five yards inside his own half, went sailing over the bar. These were two of seven penalty kicks at goal in the first twenty minutes, Kember failing with three of them for the All Blacks.

The Welsh were going great guns, with Rowlands varying his little kicks up the blind side with floating kicks up the middle. But now came our first glimpse in Britain of the promise of young Thorne in the All Blacks' centre. Herewini ran square and passed to Thorne, who was running straight. Thorne took the ball on the burst some fifteen yards inside his own half, broke inside and, running with great power, pace, and determination, scored at the posts, having beaten at least four cover tackles. Next, three minutes before halftime. Herewini grubkicked and Doug Rees gathered the ball skilfully and was overwhelmed. Kirkpatrick pounced on the loose ball and

Meads went over for a try, Kember again converting. Early in the second half Kember kicked a fine penalty goal from near touch—the All Blacks, at 13-6, seemed to have reached an unassailable lead.

It was now, however, that the fun really started for the spectators—some of whom appeared in danger of slipping, in their excitement, from the rooftop perches around the ground. First, Doug Rees kicked another penalty goal from 45 yards. Then Jones intercepted and raced away for what the locals thought was a try. Unfortunately for them, the referee ruled a knock-on. But soon, midway through the second half, West Wales heeled against the head. Rowlands came round the scrum, made a half-break, and kicked diagonally left where Kember was put under pressure by Jones. The ball went loose and H. Williams gathered it and went over for a try, converted by Doug Rees with a beautiful kick from far out, making it 14-13 to West Wales.

The crowd were now beside themselves as the Welsh held on determinedly to their one-point lead and as Rowlands, in his element, directed operations with all his old shrewd skill. Ten minutes from the end, however, New Zealand forward power told and, with Meads, Tremain, Gray, and Jennings in the lead, the All Blacks drove the ball up the field on the left. The ball came out quicky from the ruck, the direction of the thrust was switched instantly to the right, and Thorne ran over for his second try past a depleted defence. After that it was something of an anti-climax when, with two minutes left, Going nipped over for a try—from a Welsh heel out of a scrum in their 25—and Kember made the conversion.

It was a richly entertaining match, and the Welsh had put up a grand fight. They had won the heels against the put-in 5-1, and at the line-out they had won clean possession 18 times to the All Blacks' 16 with 19 inconclusive. Rowlands personally had done all that could have been expected of him, even by his most ardent fans. But what counted in the end was the mighty strength and skill of the All Blacks at the rucks. Meads must have been glad to have Ken Gray back in the side with him.

Wales's Raw Turn-Out

KEN GRAY was duly picked to play in the Test against Wales to be played at Cardiff Arms Park on Saturday, November 11. He was not, however, chosen to play at tight head, which was the position he had occupied in all his previous Tests, but at loose head, a place he had often occupied for Wellington. This was a surprise because it involved the dropping of Hazlett who had been at loose head in New Zealand's last six Tests, four against the Lions, one against Australia, and one against England. Hazlett was a more experienced prop than Muller whose only Tests were against Australia (deputising for Gray who was recovering from his knee injury) and the previous week against England. Yet it was Muller who was retained for the Test against Wales.

Many rumours started going around about this unexpected choice. It was said that New Zealand needed all Gray's strength and know-how to look after Brian Thomas who had the reputation of being the hardest lock in Britain but had for this match been chosen by Wales as tight head prop. It was said, by those who doubted the Welsh selectors' wisdom in playing Thomas out of position, that Gray had obviously been put opposite him so as to make the utmost capital from Thomas's unfamiliarity with the prop position. It was also said that Hazlett had been seen to throw a punch more or less in front of the Royal Box at Twickenham and was therefore being disciplined. The official explanation was that Muller's extra weight (17 stone compared with Hazlett's 15 stone) was essential for this match. Certainly the pack would now have an average weight of only just under 16 stone —one of the heaviest ever fielded by New Zealand.

The inclusion of Gray at the expense of Hazlett was the only change from the side which had won at Twickenham. Earlier in the week there had been doubts about the fitness of

McCormick (rib), Laidlaw (leg), and Tremain (Achilles tendon), but they were all declared fit for the match. Tremain would thus become the New Zealander with the second biggest number of appearances for his country, for this was to be his 33rd Test. It was to be Meads's 40th.

Wales had been faced with a lot of difficulties in trying to raise a worthy team. There had been two important retirements. One was that of Alun Pask, a wonderfully gifted player who, though he preferred to play at No. 8, always seemed to me best suited to the wing forward position. He had rare dexterity with both hand and foot. What a supremely constructive game he played from blind side wing forward for the Lions at Rotorua. The other retirement was that of Dewi Bebb, a very fast left wing. He had a wretched time with injuries on the Lions' 1962 tour of South Africa but happily got through Australia and New Zealand unscathed in 1966, showing elusiveness and scoring some clever tries.

Wales had also lost David Watkins, who had played stand-off half in all four of the Lions' Tests in New Zealand in 1966 as well as in the two Tests in Australia. He had turned professional for Salford. His great pace and his agility had enabled him to make a successful start in Rugby League. I felt that if someone could coach him into running straight, he would have a fine future in the professional game.

The plans of Wales and of David Nash, the national coach, had also been upset by injuries to two key players. The first of these was Keith Jarrett, who had damaged a knee. Jarrett, normally a centre, was still at school early in the previous season at the end of which Wales chose him out of position as their full-back against England because of his exceptional place-kicking. The way he went on to kick 16 points—and score a try as well—had passed into Welsh legend. Wales desperately wanted him at full-back to kick goals against New Zealand, but Mr Lewis, physiotherapist to the Welsh team, just could not get him fit in time. The other injured man was Gerald Davies, probably the most creative centre in the British Isles, who is a man the Lions could have done with as a replacement when Walsh had to go home to Cork from Sydney. Davies, too, had a knee injury. Wales had also decided to take the field without those two Lions line-out experts, Delme Thomas and Brian Price, and without Ken Jones, their Lions centre.

It was therefore an unusually raw side that Wales fielded against New Zealand. There was six newcomers, and the only section of the team in which there was a solid collection of experience was in the front row of the pack where Denzil Williams had played in three out of the four Lions Tests in New Zealand in 1966 and Gale had already hooked twenty times for Wales. Even here Thomas, winning his fifteenth cap, was playing out of position. At lock, Wiltshire was winning his first cap and Mainwaring had not got into the side until after the start of the previous season. Of the loose forwards, Taylor had been a newcomer the previous season, and Jeffery and Hughes had not played before. Behind the pack, Edwards had played only in Wales's last two games the previous season, and John only in the first two. Jones, Hall, and Wheeler were newcomers, Raybould was in his second Test season, and only Stuart Watkins, with sixteen Welsh caps and a Lions tour behind him, could be called an experienced Test player among the backs.

Wales had beaten New Zealand in 1905, 1935, and 1953, but their record in the 1966-67 season had been wretched. They had lost all their first four matches before profiting from England's mistakes and winning that extraordinary April Test, 34-21.

There were one or two notably interesting players in the Welsh side, especially Keri Jones, the 22-year-old left wing. He abandoned Rugby in 1966 in order to devote himself entirely to athletics. As a result he sprinted for Wales in the Commonwealth Games in Jamaica.

Before the match I felt that New Zealand's great advantage in experience would count for much in the emotional and heady atmosphere which prevails at the Arms Park on Test days. I thought Wales's bulky and slow-moving front row would be especially vulnerable to the rapid movement of the ball about the paddock by the All Blacks. I thought Wales's only chance lay in making as much use as possible of Welsh native wit, agility, and dexterity to try to break up the pattern of the All Blacks' play.

MATCH SIX

v. WALES
AT CARDIFF
SATURDAY, NOVEMBER 11, 1967

Wales

P. J. Wheeler (Aberavon)

S. J. Watkins (Newport), W. H. Raybould (London Welsh), I. Hall (Aberavon), W. K. Jones (Cardiff

B. John (Cardiff), G. Edwards (Cardiff)

J. J. Jeffery (Newport), J. Taylor (London Welsh), W. T. Mainwaring (Aberavon), M. Wiltshire (Aberavon) D. Hughes (Newbridge), D. Williams (Ebbw Vale), N. R. Gale (Llanelli), capt., B. E. Thomas (Neath)

New Zealand

W. F. McCormick

M. J. Dick, W. L. Davis, W. M. Birtwistle

I. R. MacRae, E. W. Kirton

C. R. Laidlaw

B. J. Lochore, capt., K. R. Tremain, S. C. Strahan, C. E. Meads, G. C. Williams, K. F. Gray, B. E. McLeod, B. L. Muller

REFEREE: M. H. TITCOMB (England)

WALES 6 POINTS

Dropped goal—John; penalty goal—Gale

NEW ZEALAND 13 POINTS

2 tries—Birtwistle, Davis; 2 conversions—McCormick; penalty goal—McCormick

Putting on the Pressure

As so often before in South Wales, the weather gods did their best and worst to upset the plans of both sides. They gathered as much sea mist from that long indented coastline and as much drizzle from the Black Mountain and its neighbours as they could possibly muster. And they hurled and funnelled it with great gusts of wind into the west end of the Arms Park from over the River Taff. Those Welsh boys who love to clamber up the goalposts before the kick-off found the dripping painted wood desperately difficult to grip. Those who delight in throwing toilet rolls found the paper soon became too saturated and heavy to be whisked from one end of the paddock to the other.

But no wind or rain will ever stop the Welsh from singing. They stood there, banked up and bunched in their thousands, soaking and getting more soaked, yet happy and singing 'Land of my Fathers' with a fervour never to be surpassed by any other sporting crowd. To withstand the emotion of these moments a player needs a nerve of iron. One new Welsh player told me he could not possibly have held a pass had he been given one in the first ten minutes. He did not feel level-headed until the interval. This is where experience counts.

To the dismay of many Welshmen their captain, Gale, decided to give New Zealand first use of the wind. The Welsh had early encouragement, however, when, after three minutes, Gray was adjudged offside at a maul. The New Zealanders did not retire 10 yards, and Wheeler was called up to take a long penalty kick at goal. Sadly for his well-wishers, his kick hardly lifted the ball off the ground, and New Zealand were soon making their presence felt. They maintained a mighty shove when Wales put the ball into a set scrum with the result that the Welsh heel was fatally slowed.

More worries for the Welsh came in the seventh and tenth

minutes. First Edwards had his left hand trodden on and crushed. Then, while the All Blacks held the ball in a set scrum, Raybould—moving quickly to take up a fresh defensive position to counter a switch in position by the New Zealand backs—walked in front of the hindmost foot of his pack, thus giving McCormick a simple penalty goal (3-0).

A fleeting chance came and went for Wales two minutes later. Laidlaw was overwhelmed by Wales when the ball went untidily from a line-out. A set scrum was called with Wales to put in, but John's dropkick at goal went wide. This was followed by a lecture to the two front rows from the referee—a strange system of appointments meant that this was the same man who had refereed the All Blacks the previous Wednesday —after which he awarded a penalty to New Zealand.

Next came two brilliant pieces of New Zealand back play, defying the treacherous footholds and the wet and slippery ball. While Kirton ran to the left and open side, Laidlaw passed instead direct to MacRae who had come round behind the forwards. McCormick came in as well on the blind side, and Dick was given a run. Nothing came directly of this, but a minute later a set scrum not far from the Welsh posts suddenly swung round and the ball came out from the Welsh pack for the use of the New Zealand backs. Laidlaw promptly sent it out leftwards, MacRae passed it on, Davis slipped through Hall's defence, and Birtwistle just got over in the left-hand corner. McCormick converted with a kick of which Don Clarke, not to mention Mick Williment, would have been mighty proud (8-0).

New Zealand were soon attacking again and once Wales, in order to clear their lines, got Keri Jones to lob the ball over the top of a mini line-out direct to John who found touch. In the last ten minutes before halftime, McCormick had two unsuccessful penalty kicks at goal for New Zealand. Edwards made a nice run on the blind side for Wales, only to see his pass to Stuart Watkins dropped. As the interval approached, the ball went astray behind a Welsh line-out, and Williams almost managed to touch it down for a try.

The arguments will no doubt rage for a long long time in the valleys of South Wales about whether Wales were right or wrong to give New Zealand first use of the wind. The guiding principle in these matters is to take for your own side whatever the elements are offering from the start. In this instance Gale could always answer that, in spite of the help from the wind, New Zealand led only 8-0 at the interval. Moreover Wales, had they been successful with their kicks of the first half and with those which were to come to them in the second half, could have won with something to spare.

For a while after the interval it looked as if Gale's plan might just work. Edwards and John both sent high kicks up into the swirling wind and rain, and a too powerful New Zealand heel from a set scrum sent the ball direct to Kirton who was overwhelmed. This led to a series of set scrums near the New Zealand line, from one of which, after nine minutes of the second half, John dropped a goal when Keri Jones passed the ball to him from a set scrum, a ragged heel having deceived Edwards (8-3).

Soon after this, however, the tide took a sudden crucial turn against Wales. They were penalised at a set scrum, and New Zealand decided to barge their way ahead from a tapped penalty, rather like Rugby League forwards from a play-the-ball. While this was going on, the referee caught Mainwaring grappling with Muller, and this time Lochore gave the ball to McCormick for a long kick at goal. The ball fell short of the posts, but Jeffery first fumbled his catch and then sent the ball wildly behind him. Amid the general confusion Davis raced in for a try near the posts which McCormick converted (13-3).

This looked like the end for Wales, but in the space of the next ten minutes they had four chances of scoring. Stuart Watkins actually got over the New Zealand line but was prevented from grounding the ball. Wheeler failed with a long penalty kick at goal. Edwards was given a long penalty kick at goal, but he also failed. Wheeler tried yet again to kick a penalty goal, this time from inside his own half. Eventually, after MacRae had been shaken by a tackle by Edwards and after New Zealand had themselves used a mini line-out to clear their lines, the All Blacks were penalised at a ruck. Gale, despairing of finding a reliable goalkicker, performed the deed himself (13-6).

There were still 13 minutes to go, but it was now too late for Wales to save themselves. John tried a last Garryowen, but McCormick stood firm and marked it. Wiltshire charged ahead from a tap at a line-out, but the All Blacks stopped him and promptly won the ruck for Laidlaw. Twice in quick succession Lochore's pack checked a heel at a set scrum and walked the Welsh back and back and back with such control and contempt as I had not seen since the day the Lions played poor Delme Thomas in the front row in the third Test at Christchurch. Here, as there, they proved who were the real masters.

There were those, of course, who said that Wales had thrown the game away. It is true that five Welsh kicks at goal went astray, that the penalty goal caused by Raybould was something of a gift to New Zealand, and that both New Zealand tries owed much to Welsh errors. But it would be fairer to say that when a pack of forwards are applying such pressure as the All Backs were at the set scrums and rucks, any subsequent errors by their opponents should be credited to those who have been applying the pressure.

The All Blacks played hard, sensible, controlled, and balanced Rugby, realistically styled to suit the conditions. They gave us a few glimpses of the attacking skill of their backs—just as many as the conditions allowed—and both Laidlaw and Kirton kicked with fine precision and variety. I thought New Zealand owed a great deal to these two, and the value of a long-established partnership between halfback and first five-eighth was seldom more clearly demonstrated. Even in the wind and rain, Laidlaw's long, spun pass, boring through the drizzle, almost always went exactly where Kirton wanted it. Similarly, when Kirton saw the ball was coming out awkwardly from the forwards, he would sense his partner's difficulties and instantly move into a position to which Laidlaw would have only to shovel, almost just to nudge, the ball to him. Some of Laidlaw's passing was as quick as that of Ken Catchpole, of Australia, and his understanding with Kirton was in the rare Catchpole-Hawthorne class.

The Brothers Camberabero

NEXT DAY, Sunday, November 12, the All Blacks took off to fly over the Channel and across France to Lyons, there to meet South-east France on the Wednesday in the first of their four matches in France. Tremain was still troubled by his Achilles tendon, Laidlaw and Birtwistle both had thigh trouble, and MacRae had his right eye almost closed as a result of the heavy tackle from Edwards at Cardiff. In any case, this match at Lyons provided a good opportunity for giving the non-Test players in the party a game. Of the fifteen who beat Wales only Lochore, Meads, and McLeod were to play at Lyons.

French Rugby at this time was enlivened by one of these theoretical battles between styles and methods which add so much to its attraction. During the previous season's home internationals—or Tournament of Five Nations, as the French call it—France had for once abandoned their highly entertaining flowing open Rugby. In its place was a much more static game based on hard forward play, supported by the kicking of the Camberabero brothers at halfback. They had built up a pack of solid scrummagers. And from behind them, one or other of the Camberaberos—usually Guy, the stand-off—would kick either for touch or for goal. Before the Camberabero brothers were brought into the side, France lost 8-9 to Scotland in Paris. But with the brothers in harness, France beat Australia 20-14 in Paris, England 16-12 at Twickenham, Wales 20-14 in Paris, and Ireland 11-6 in Dublin. The part played by the Camberaberos in these victories can be seen from the number of points they scored. Against Australia, the brothers contributed all France's 20 points. Guy kicked four penalty goals, dropped a goal and made a conversion, and Lilian scored the try. Against England, Guy kicked 10 of France's 16 points, against Wales 14 out of 20, and against Ireland eight out of 11.

France duly won the championship, and there was great rejoicing. At the same time, however, many Frenchmen were sad that this triumph had been gained at the expense of the gay, quick, colourful Rugby for which France had been so much admired throughout the world. The seeds which were to grow into the Battle of the Styles had been sown.

In the close season France had to fulfil their commitments in South Africa, deputising for the All Blacks. It was not a successful tour as far as the results of the four Tests went. South Africa won the first Test 26-3 and the second 16-3. France managed to win the third 19-14, and the fourth was drawn 6-6. Of the 13 matches, the French won eight and lost four. There was a great deal of adverse criticism in the French Press of both the planning of the tour and of the management of it by Monsieur Marcel Laurent, who had also managed the French tour of New Zealand in 1961. It was unfortunate for Guy Camberabero that his brother, the scrum-half, was not available for the tour. Guy needed his brother's immensely long passes to put him clear of any opponents who might try to charge down his kicks.

The controversy surrounding this tour of South Africa gave impetus to the supporters of the fluid game in their theoretical and verbal skirmishes against the supporters of the static game. The fluid people had always held that Guy Camberabero positioned himself in such a way that a proper three-quarter movement was impossible. They had said that the Rugby which had won the Five Nations' Tournament was ugly and un-French. Now, pointing at the Test results, they said it was not even efficient. They, who had been fervent supporters of the type of creative open football as practised by André and Guy Boniface, that princely pair of centres, now demanded that Guy Camberabero should be replaced by little Jean Gachassin, of Lourdes.

The All Blacks may not have known it, but they walked right into the middle of this battle and themselves helped to decide the issue. The French have never liked trial matches as such, and so the French selectors decided that the first two matches the All Blacks were to play in France, at Lyons and Toulouse, would be used for the sifting of the different talent available to the selectors. At Lyons, in the first match, they would see the Camberabero brothers. At Toulouse, in the second match, they would see Gachassin who, even the supporters of the static had to admit, had an exceptional eye for an opening and a gift for making a half-opening. Thus it was that the team the All Blacks were to play at Lyons, and which was labelled 'South-east', included several players who had nothing whatever to do with that region. Perhaps the selectors of the North of England side were not all that inconsistent after all!

The French plans were somewhat upset by the withdrawal from the South-east team of Lilian Camberabero, the scrum-half, because of injury. Even so the dice seemed loaded in his brother's favour, and against Gachassin, because the French pack of forwards for the Lyons match was on paper very much stronger than that chosen for Toulouse, where Gachassin was to show his paces. The pack for this first match at Lyons, in fact, included five Test players. Gruarin and Berejnoi had been France's regular props for the last four seasons. Herrero, now at No. 8, had played in that position and at lock and wing forward for his country since 1964 when he played against the 1963–64 All Blacks. And Carrere, though he had only one season of Test Rugby behind him, had looked the natural successor to that fearsome wing forward, Michel Crauste. In addition, Plantefol had had great success as a line-out jumper on the recent French tour of South Africa. The only other back with a reputation was Maso, a gifted centre but one who had been injured in his only Test, and had apparently been thought too fragile to take to South Africa. The All Blacks therefore had two things to worry about: the strength of the South-east's pack and the boot of Guy Camberabero.

New Zealand Rugby Touring Team 1967
Back row: *P. H. Clarke, W. D. Cottrell, W. M. Birtwistle, G. F. Kember, W. J. Nathan, G. C. Williams, M. C. Wills, B. E. McLeod, A. G. Steel*
Second row: *E. J. Hazlett, K. R. Tremain, I. A. Kirkpatrick, K. F. Gray, C. E. Meads, S. C. Strahan, A. E. Hopkinson, A. G. Jennings, B. L. Muller*   Sitting: *W. L. Davis, M. J. Dick, S. M. Going, I. R. MacRae (Vice-Captain), C. K. Saxton (Manager), B. J. Lochore (Captain), F. R. Allen (Assistant Manager), G. S. Thorne, E. W. Kirton, J. Major, W. F. McCormick   In front: C. R. Laidlaw, M. A. Herewini.*

Photo: FRANK THOMPSON

The coach, rapping out his orders, begins at the beginning. Fred Allen, wearing a Lions jersey, seeks perfection in basic binding and scrummaging while his charges sweat it out under his merciless eye at Wilmslow in preparation for the first match of the tour.

TOPIX

All eyes on the ball as Going gets it away unmolested from a line-out at Manchester. All Blacks, from left to right, are Nathan, Lochore (kneeling), McLeod, Hazlett, and Muller. North of England players, from left to right, are Pickering, Greenwood, Coulman, and Lansbury (2), who clearly has been allowed little chance to harass Going.

Bob Taylor poised in distributing the ball won by the gallant Counties pack at Leicester. Lochore (right), Laidlaw, and Major watch keenly to see where the next phase of play will be. The Counties players, from left to right, are

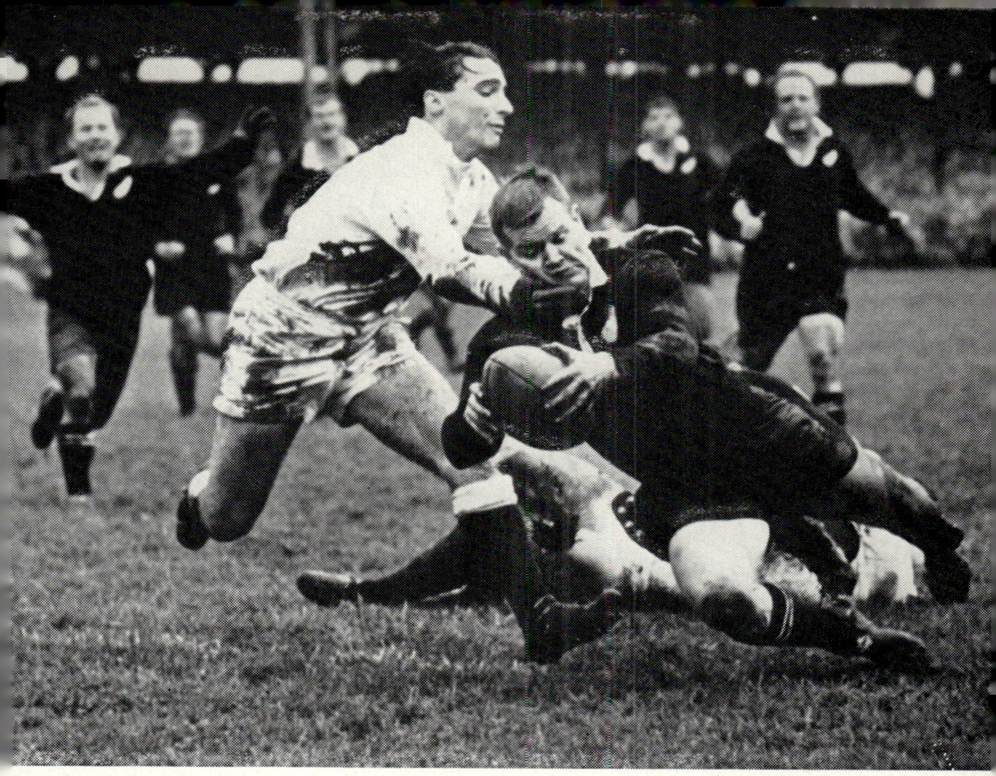

TOPIX

Above: Tony Steel plunges over for a try at Bristol although risking decapitation at the hands of Starmer-Smith. Going (left) throws up his hands in delight.

Below: If Sid Going spots a gap, he needs no urging. Here he begins a typical break close to his pack at Bristol. He will not lack support. His forwards are already wrenching themselves free.

BRISTOL UNITED PRESS

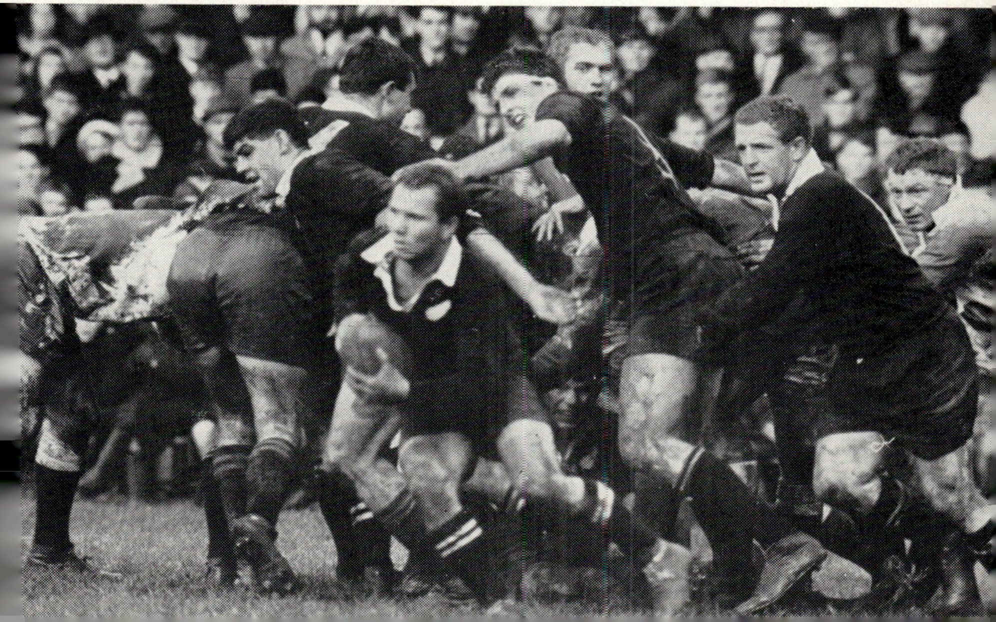

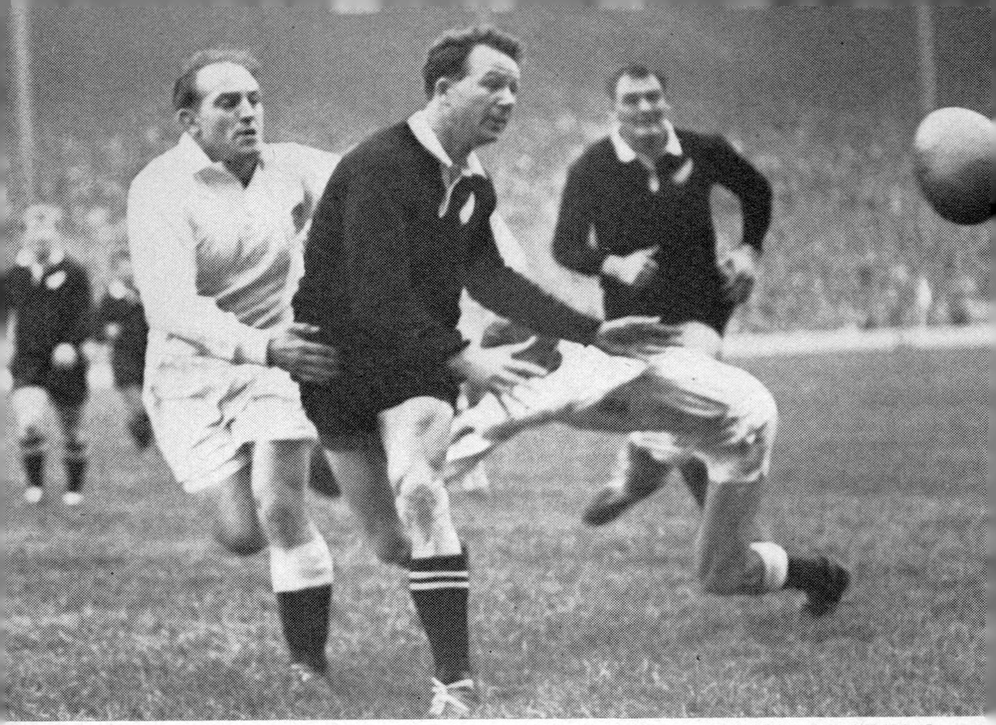

Pictures by SPORT AND GENERAL

Above: Ian MacRae straightens up and draws two England players on to himself before passing the ball out at Twickenham. Lochore is not far behind in support. The England player on the left is Godwin.

Below: John Owen (No. 5), who looks as if he may be offside, tries to prevent Kel Tremain from getting the ball back to Laidlaw (9) in the England Test at Twickenham. The All Blacks supporting Tremain are, left to right, Hazlett, Meads, Strahan, and Lochore. The other England players are Larter (headband), Horton, and Gittings (behind Horton).

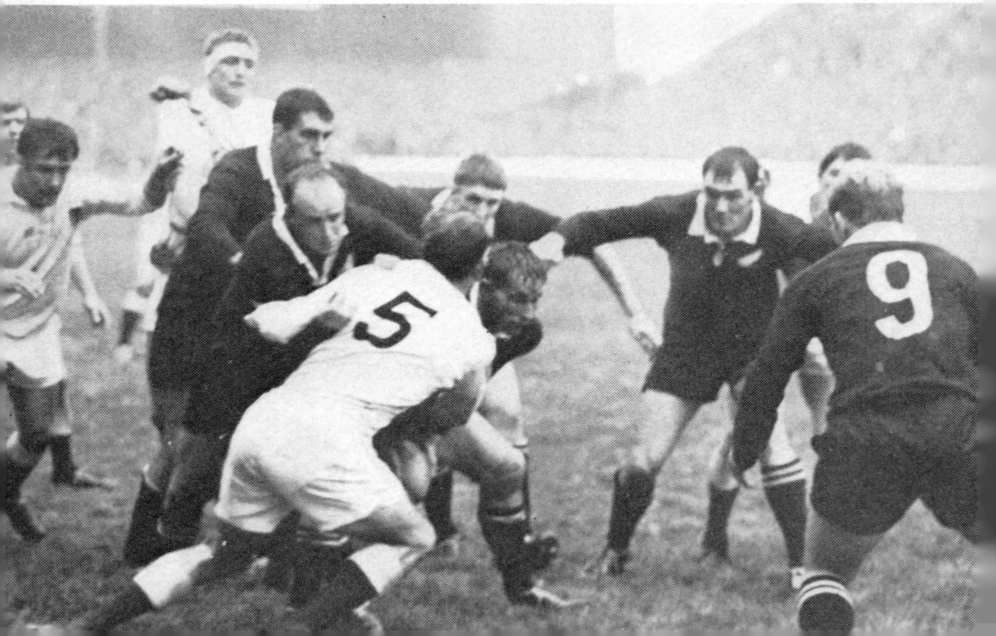

Above: Earl Kirton slides over just inside the corner flag for one of his two tries against England. Birtwistle is separated from him by the flag-post, and Savage looks a trifle angry or dismayed or perhaps both. Rutherford watches from the ground, and Horton picks himself up.

Below: While Owen (5) and Meads still grapple with each other, Bert Godwin furtively takes the ball away from a line-out for England at Twickenham. McLeod, left, prepares to interfere. The other England players, left to right, are Larter, Gittings, Rogers, and Taylor.

The Meads Incident

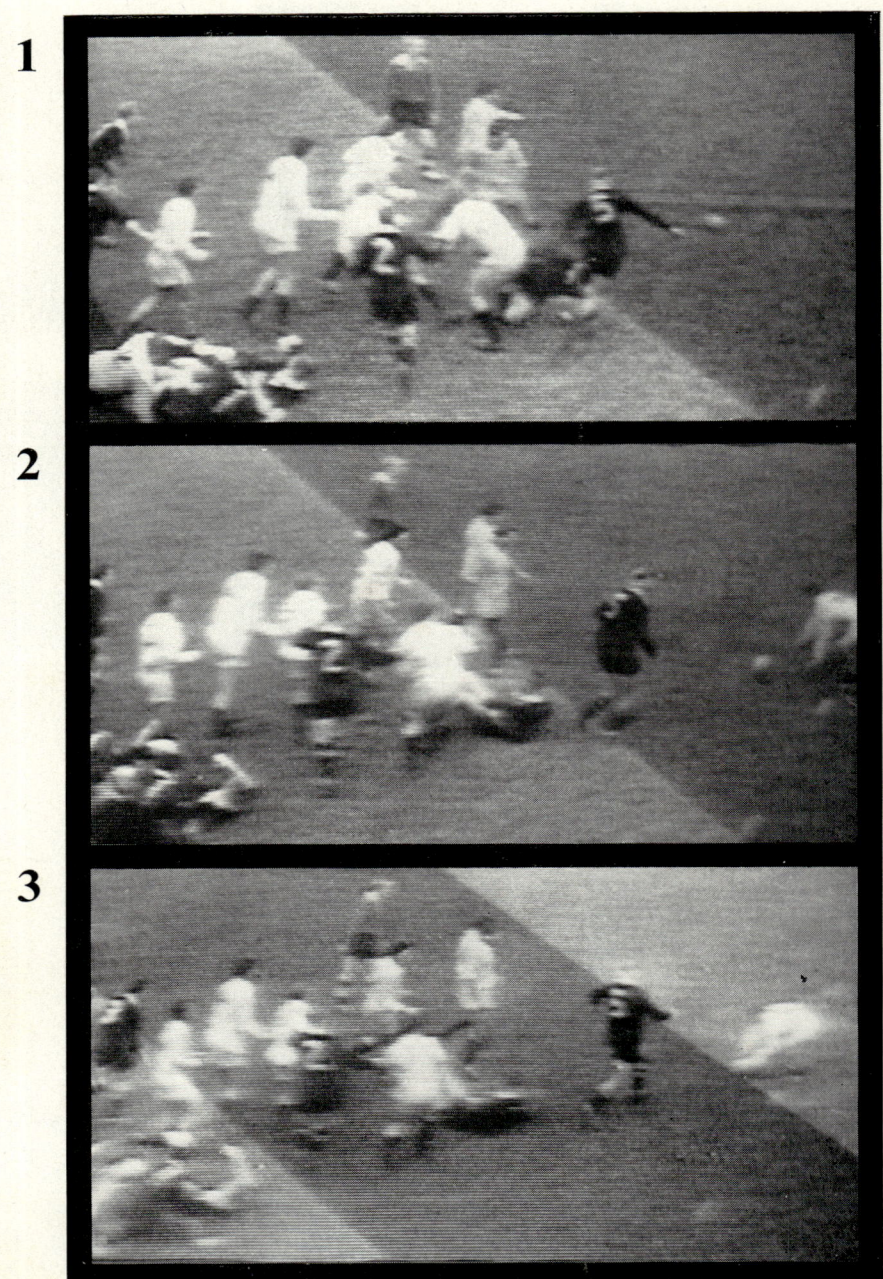

Was it dangerous play or was it not? Readers can judge for themselves from the evidence of this sequence of pictures from B.B.C. Television News. Or does the camera lie?

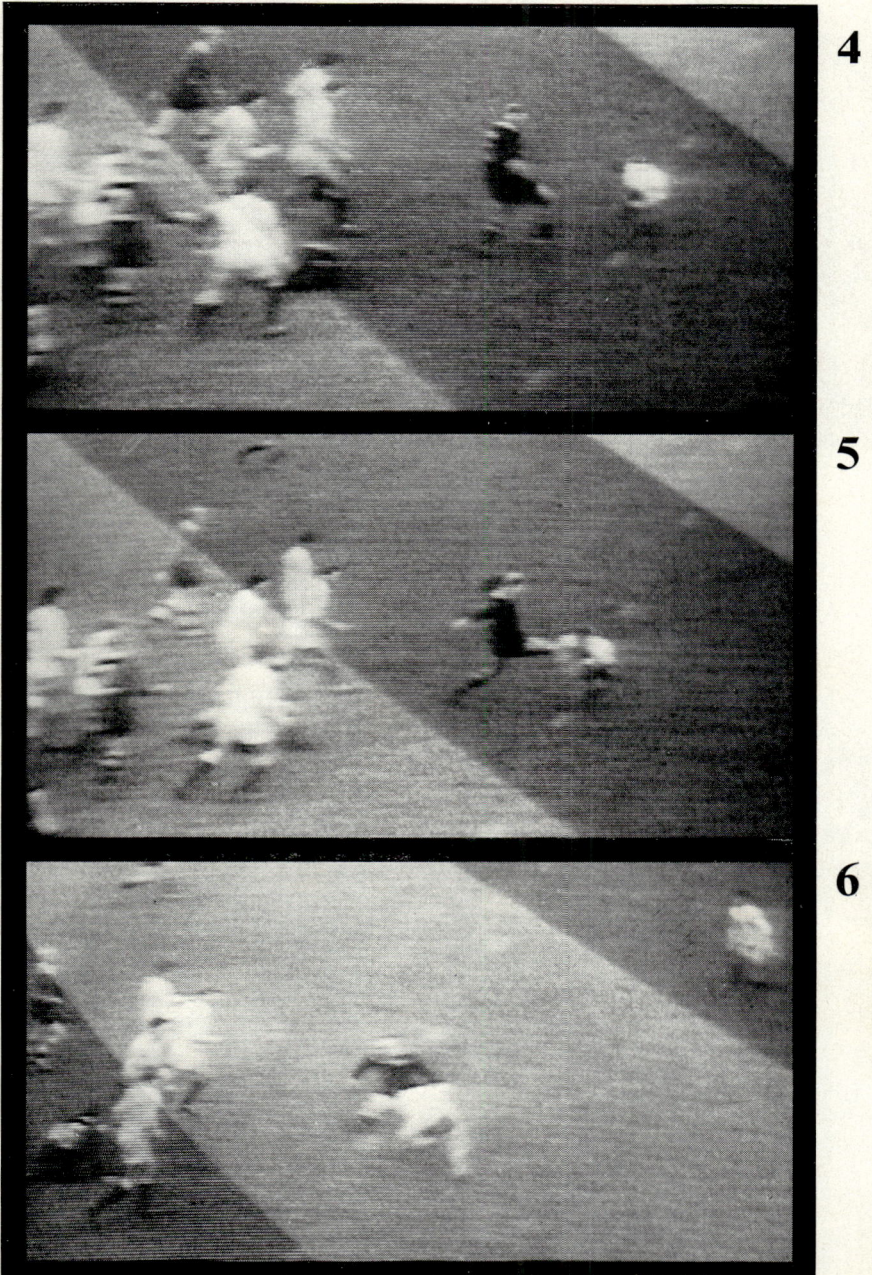

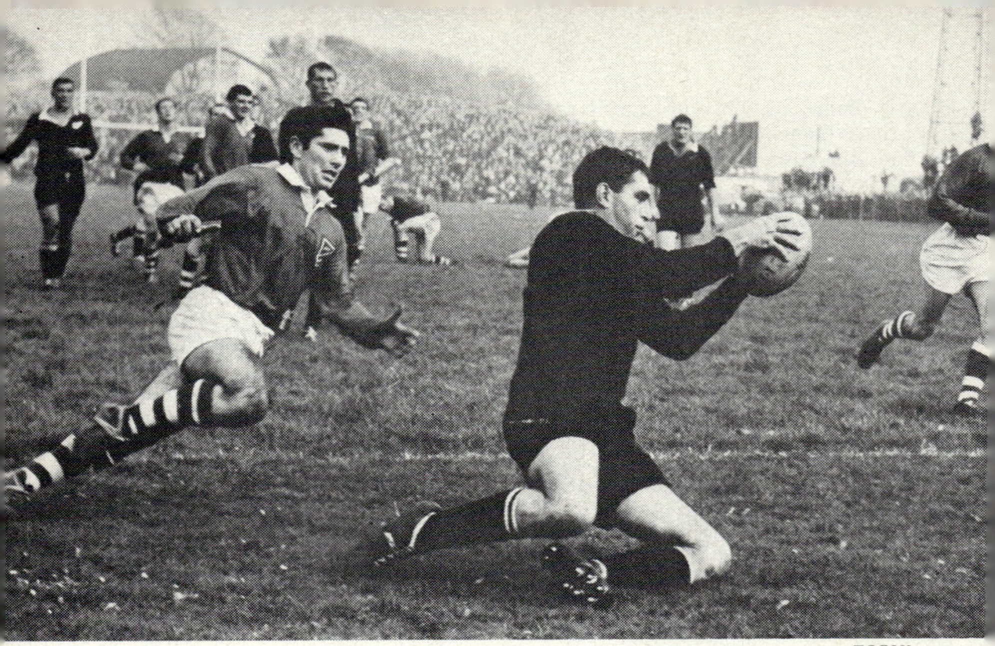

TOPIX

Above: Colin Meads, captaining the All Blacks against West Wales at Swansea, scores his only try of the tour.

Below: Howard Rees, the West Wales wing threequarter, tries to take a ball knocked down at the front of a line-out at Swansea, but John Major intervenes. Under Rees's armpit can be seen the bandaged hand of Gray, playing his first game after injury. He seems oblivious of the hand of Delme Thomas laid upon his shoulder.

TOPIX

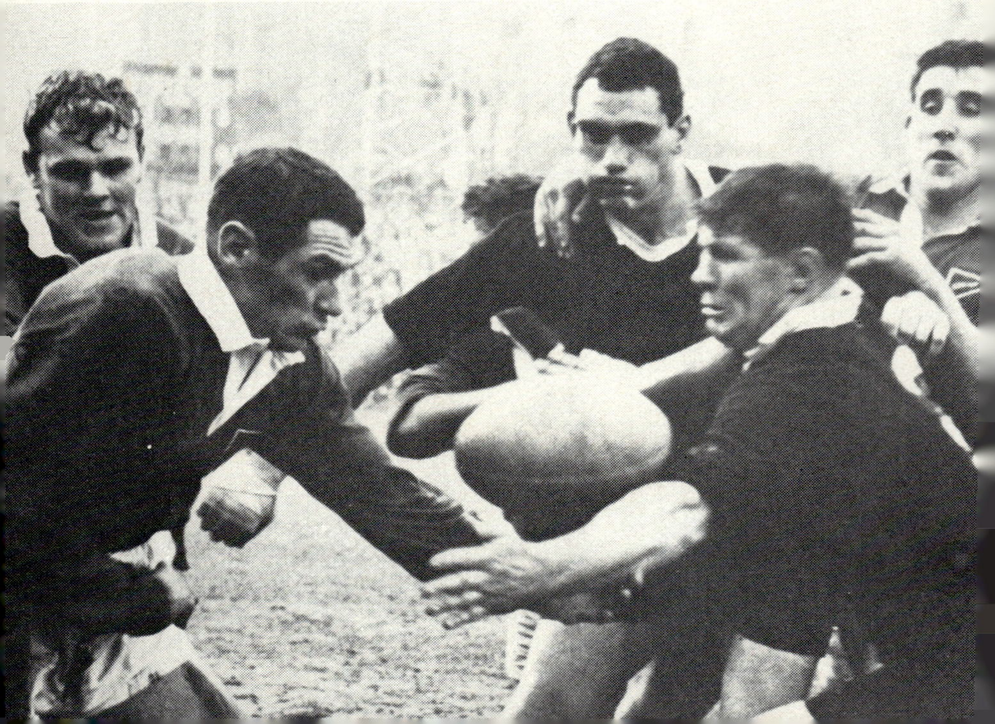

TOPIX

Two ways of dealing with a loose ball. The ball has come down on the Welsh side of a line-out in the Wales-New Zealand game at Cardiff, and while Gareth Edwards, left, prepares to gather it, Brian Thomas arrives to kill it. The other players, left to right, are Taylor, Lochore, Jeffery, Wiltshire, Hughes, Gale, Meads, Tremain, Mainwaring, and Williams.

The ballet comes to Lyons, but the ball sails high above Faletto's graceful leap at this line-out. Kirkpatrick or Lochore, at the back, seem more likely to catch it. The South-East France players, from left to right, are Lartigue (9), Yachvili (partly hidden), Carrere, Herrero (beard), Plantefol, Berejnoi (blocking?), Faletto (ballet), Gruarin (protecting Faletto from Meads?), and Robert (2). One of the bulldozers and some of its achievements can be seen in the background.

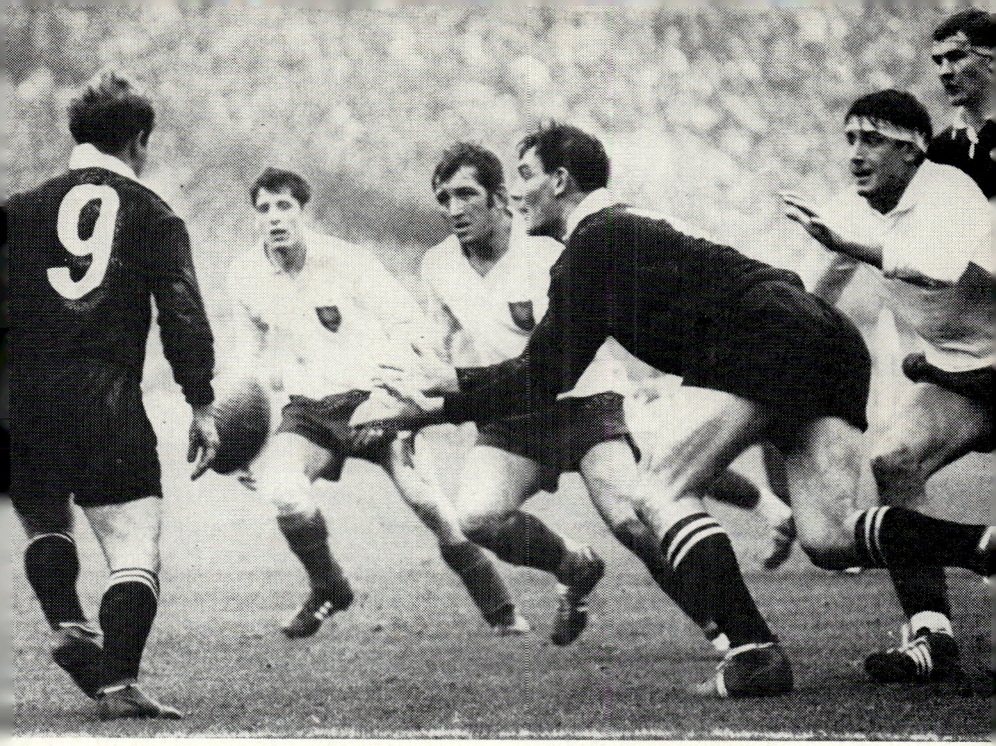

UNITED PRESS INTERNATIONAL

Above: Strength and artistry are combined in this sweeping pass by Brian Lochore against France at Colombes. Going, left, and Kirkpatrick, right, watch admiringly. The French players, left to right, are Quilis, Cabanier, and Plantefol.

Below: How's that for a ruck, Fred? Surely even Fred Allen, the perfectionist coach, would approve of this rucking technique as Waka Nathan lets the ball out in front of the Scottish District's posts at Melrose.

THE SCOTSMAN

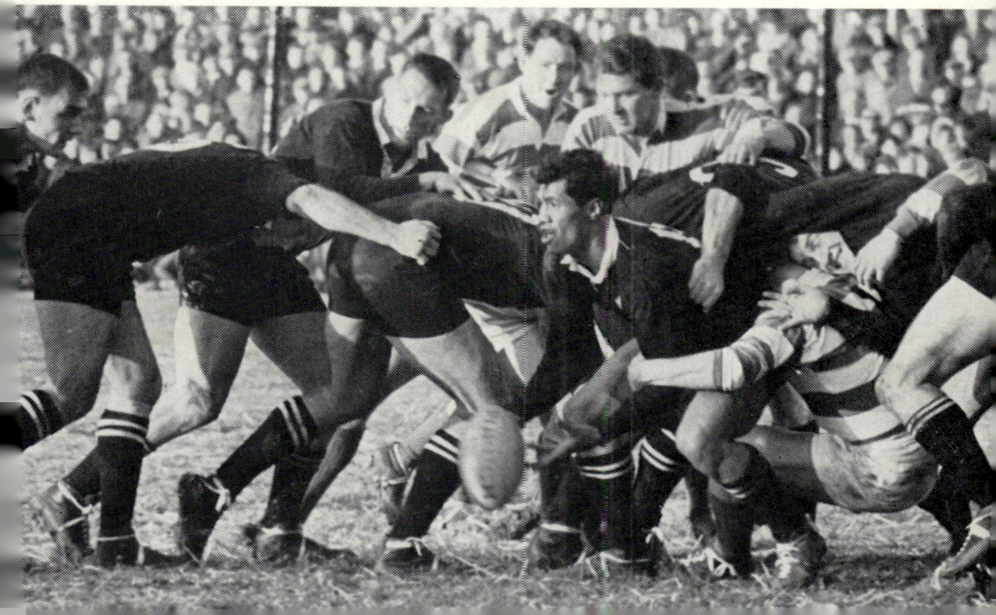

Sid Going prepares to crosskick as four Monmouthshire players, two 1966 Lions among them, close in on him at Newport. The two Lions are Brian Price, his middle hidden by the ball, and Denzil Williams, right background.

The All Blacks lost their 100 per cent victory record when East Wales held them to a 3-3 draw at Cardiff. The crowd's enjoyment of the game can be judged by this mobbing of the teams as they leave the field.

Airborne Barbarians halfback Gareth Edwards passes the ball out as C. R. Laidlaw clamps a hand on the seat of his shorts in the match at Twickenham.

MATCH SEVEN

v. SOUTH-EAST FRANCE
AT LYONS
WEDNESDAY, NOVEMBER 15, 1967

South-East France

D. Laprade (Valance)

A. Besseat (Grenoble), H. Etchart (Aurillac), J. Maso (Perpignan), J. J. Lenient (Vichy)

G. Camberabero (La Voulte), J. Lartigue (Avignon)

A. Herrero (Toulon), capt., C. Carrere (Toulon), A. Plantefol (Agen), J. Faletto (Valence), M. Yachvili (Tulle), J. C. Berejnoi (Tulle), J. Robert (Angouleme), A. Gruarin (Toulon)

All Blacks

G. F. Kember

A. G. Steel, G. S. Thorne, P. H. Clarke

W. D. Cottrell, M. A. Herewini

S. M. Going

B. J. Lochore, capt., M. C. Wills, A. E. Smith, C. E. Meads, I. A. Kirkpatrick, E. J. Hazlett, B. E. McLeod, A. E. Hopkinson

REFEREE: H. B. LAIDLAW (Scotland)

SOUTH-EAST FRANCE 3 POINTS

Dropped goal—G. Camberabero

ALL BLACKS 16 POINTS

4 tries—McLeod, Steel (2), Kirkpatrick; 2 conversions—Kember

Swinging in the Rain

EVERYBODY IN BRITAIN who appreciated the skill and determination with which the All Blacks had overcome the effects of the wretched weather on their efforts to play fluent Rugby, hoped and believed that in France at least they would find firm ground and a dry ball so that they could really fulfil their potential. It was not to be—not yet at least. For the rain started coming down shortly before the kick-off at Lyons. And, except for one brief period, it went on coming down all through the game, increasing to a downpour.

In spite of the appalling weather and the fact that parts of the stadium were being bulldozed—making it look, someone said, as if a lawn had suddenly been put down in the middle of a lunar crater—there was a crowd of about 20,000 to see the French pack in the first half give just the kind of tough, solid display expected of them.

The All Blacks indeed were under a lot of pressure in the first half, and more than 20 minutes went by before there was a set scrum or a line-out in the French half. One moment the highly excitable crowd were expressing shrill disagreement with the decisions of the Scottish referee. The next, they were cheering madly as Gruarin—easily distinguishable even in this gloomy light by his thick black moustache—hurtled into the All Blacks' 25 with the ball tucked under one arm.

It was not until the 26th minute that the All Blacks scored their first try, and it came significantly from the first of their four heels against the head. Going ran off with the ball. And after Kirkpatrick and Hopkinson had handled, McLeod was put over in the corner. A minute later the noisy crowd went wild with delight as the South-east swept the All Blacks back over their line for what looked as if it might be a try. But the referee was not satisfied and ordered a scrum-five. Now the French tried to score through their loose forwards, but this move too failed, and there was another set scrum. This time Lartigue sent out a quick pass to Camberabero—who promptly dropped the goal that everybody was expecting.

The South-east were holding their own splendidly, and just before halftime they very nearly scored again. A counter-attack launched by Maso was continued by the French pack with Faletto prominent, but the slippery ball just eluded Besseat at the line. It was a near thing. And the All Blacks had plenty to look anxious about during the interval.

Immediately afterwards, however, the game swung suddenly in the All Blacks' favour. Herewini's kick-off for the start of the second half led to a ruck from which Going kicked the ball towards the touchline. There Laprade, who otherwise made very few mistakes at full-back, slipped on the muddy paddock and missed the ball. Steel came racing up, grabbed the ball on the bounce, and ran the 20 yards to the French line for a try which Kember converted (8-3).

A second slap in the face followed immediately for the French. Their kick-off, following this score, went to Meads who saw a chance of a run. He charged ahead, a ruck formed, Lochore got the ball, Hazlett gave it to Kirkpatrick, and Kirkpatrick finished a long and fast run with a try in the corner which Kember converted with an excellent kick (13-3). The French never recovered from this double blow. Although they battled on bravely enough, they played as if they knew they were beaten. The All Blacks tried to play fluent Rugby, but the ball was desperately difficult to control.

The All Blacks did manage one more try however. A fine movement by the backs put Steel outside his man, and although the French cover caught him, a line-out followed from which Going put Steel over close to the touchline. Steel had a notably good game for the All Blacks as though determined to win back a place in the Test team against France ten days later. In spite of the rain, his handling was more reliable than it had often been in the past. Kirkpatrick too was clearly in healthy form, as was Going. The All Blacks had also restricted Camberabero to one dropped goal, which was a point not to be missed by the supporters of the Fluid Game.

Two Strong Sides

BEFORE LEAVING Lyons by air, the All Blacks announced a strong side for their match against France B at Toulouse on Saturday, November 18. Ten of those who had played against Wales at Cardiff the previous weekend were included. Laidlaw and Tremain, who had been advised by Mr Lewis the Welsh physiotherapist, not to play for at least ten days, were given a further break. Their places at halfback and flanker were taken by Going and Kirkpatrick. Major was given a Saturday match, Jennings came in at lock in place of Strahan, and Steel was on the left wing instead of Birtwistle. MacRae went down with flu, and Cottrell was called in to deputise at second five-eighth.

Toulouse, a big and busy industrial city with a population of 330,000, contained many English-speaking people because the Concorde airliner, a joint Anglo-French project, was being constructed in the city by Sud-Aviation. The All Blacks were given the opportunity of visiting the factory. It was also at Toulouse that Chris Laidlaw heard that he had been awarded his Rhodes Scholarship to Oxford. Nathan, with his broken jaw, found himself in good company—there was a congress of dentists going on in the All Blacks' hotel. In fact he had the apparatus removed from his jaw on the Friday but was advised not to play until the All Blacks got to Scotland.

France B are theoretically France's second team, but on this occasion they included six men who had played in Tests against the home countries and three who had been on the French tour of South Africa. The six who had played against the home countries were Villepreux, at full back; Lux and Mir, two young centres who had played for France the previous season; Campaes, the left wing who had won one cap in 1965; Gachassin, who at 5 ft. 4 in. had started his international career in 1961 as a wing threequarter but had since been chosen also at stand-off half, centre, and as an attacking full back (against Australia); and Rupert, a wing forward who had been playing for France off and on since 1964. Rupert and Gachassin were the only two players in the side aged more than 25, and Rupert was given the captaincy.

The three who had been to South Africa but had not yet played against the home countries were Quilis, at wing forward, Cardebat, at tight head prop, and Plantefol who had already played against the All Blacks at lock in the Lyons game earlier the same week. Plantefol, in fact, was brought into the France B team only as a late replacement. It was a fortunate chance for him to prove his match fitness, because he had been forced to play all his football so far that season in his club's second team. This was because he had recently changed clubs from the Racing Club in Paris to Agen in the South, and had therefore been granted only a second class licence by the French Rugby Federation.

Every French player has to have a licence which is like an identity card or small passport with details of the player's age, weight, height etc., and includes a photograph. The licences of all players are given to the referee before a club game, and he can refuse to return one if he thinks the player has let the game down. When a player wants to change clubs, his licence has to be sent to the Federation for approval of the change. Objections can be made by the former club, and the whole matter of the reason for the transfer is gone into. It is normal practice then for the player to be granted only a second class licence, as in the case of Plantefol. After a season or so he is usually granted a first-class licence again and can play for his club's first team. The idea, of course, is to discourage the transfer of players for suspect motives.

Clearly it would have been an almost impossible leap for Plantefol from his club's second team straight into France's Test team. Yet there was strong feeling in French Rugby circles that the line-out ability he had shown in South Africa was indispensable for the Test against New Zealand. Hence these two preliminary games against the All Blacks to help him to bridge the gap and to adjust his play to the pace and rhythm of top-class Rugby.

The strength of this France B side was in its backs. It was

a good idea of the selectors to give Gachassin his regular club halfback partner. This meant that four of the backs came from the Lourdes club famous for Jean Prat, Maurice Prat, Martine, Rancoule, the Labazuy brothers, the Lacaze brothers, Crauste and many other talented players who have put the emphasis first and foremost on attack.

Capendeguy, the fast right wing, has an amusing story told about him. Apparently he could not make the trip for France's match against Portugal the previous season. So he sent a telegram to the secretary of the Federation expressing his regret. Unfortunately, in the absent-minded way which apparently characterises everything he does in life except the scoring of tries, he simply signed the telegram with his first names, Jean-Michel. Now it so happened that the French full-back for this match in Portugal had the surname Michel—and the selectors naturally assumed that it was he who had cried off. They therefore hastily summoned another full-back to Portugal. To their surprise they there found Michel, the original full-back, perfectly fit and professing total ignorance of any telegram. By the time the penny had dropped it was too late and France had to play a full-back at wing threequarter.

What a pity, I felt as I fought my way through the garlic of the seething crowds towards the Toulouse stadium, what a pity that Gachassin and his merry men would not get a chance to delight us today. The France B forwards on paper looked just too lacking in experience to stand up to the tough pack the All Blacks were fielding for this match.

MATCH EIGHT

v. FRANCE B
AT TOULOUSE
SATURDAY, NOVEMBER 18, 1967

France B

P. Villepreux (Toulouse)

J-M. Capendeguy (Begles), J-P Lux (Tyrosse),
J-P. Mir (Lourdes), A. Campaes (Lourdes)

J. Gashassin (Lourdes), J-H. Mir (Lourdes)

F. Bourgade (Montauban), J-J. Rupert
(Tyrosse), capt., A. Plantefol (Agen), S. Morel
(Toulouse), A. Quilis (Narbonne), B. Garet
(Racing Club), J-P. Baux (Lannemezan), B.
Cardebat (Montauban)

All Blacks

W. F. McCormick

M. J. Dick, W. L. Davis, A. G. Steel

W. D. Cottrell, E. W. Kirton

S. M. Going

B. J. Lochore, capt., G. C. Williams, A. G.
Jennings, C. E. Meads, I. A. Kirkpatrick, K. F.
Gray, J. Major, B. L. Muller

REFEREE: G. C. LAMB (England)

FRANCE B 19 POINTS

2 tries—Plantefol, Lux; 3 penalty goals—Villepreux;
2 conversions—Villepreux

ALL BLACKS 32 POINTS

5 tries—Williams (2), Dick, Going, Kirkpatrick;
dropped goal—Cottrell; 4 conversions—McCormick;
2 penalty goals—McCormick

Fast, Heady and Breathless

AT LAST the All Blacks had the weather they wanted. The sun was shining, the foothold was firm, the ball was bone-dry and the wind, though violent at times, was yet warm and welcoming. The huge Municipal Stadium, outside the city across the broad River Garonne, is a vast unbroken concrete oval with continuous roofing all the way round. On the top of this roofing at regular intervals were from ten to twenty flagpoles, and from each of these a large red, white, and blue tricolour was straining in the breeze. Long before the two teams came up through the dark tunnel into the brilliant sunlight the gay and lively crowd was alternately cheering and booing a curtain-raiser between two uninhibited local junior sides. Compared with this—and with that strange scent of damp concrete and French cigarettes—Cardiff seemed a solemn, formal place.

Morel got the ball superbly for the French from the first line-out of the game, and the All Blacks wheeled the first set scrum. They took the ball on at their feet. Bourgade was injured in trying to stop the breakthrough, and the crowd had their first chance to hiss, boo and shout their curses at the All Blacks. Lochore stood out of a set scrum and sent the ball out to Cottrell, but the pass was forward. Then McCormick was short with a penalty kick from just inside the French half. Gachassin tried to run the ball out but dropped it, and a Frenchman had to clear hurriedly. The clearance failed to find touch, but McCormick missed goal with a long returning dropkick.

It was a hectic start. And there was no respite until, after eight minutes, Cottrell grabbed a loose ball and let fly a powerful dropkick which sent the ball high up between the posts for the first three points of the game. Capendeguy showed his pace in harassing McCormick after a diagonal kick by Gachassin. After fourteen minutes Villepreux had his first penalty kick at goal for an offence by the All Blacks at a line-out. The All Blacks had chosen to have the wind behind them. Villepreux decided the wind against him was so strong he would have to get Garet to place the ball for him. This he did, and the kick went only just wide.

The All Blacks returned to the attack straight away and whipped the ball out to Steel who turned inside his man, raced on, but was covered. Next Davis, going at a great pace, bumped off J-P. Mir in the centre and Dick was given a run. He too was covered, but then Gray ran leftwards from a line-out on the right and handed a Frenchman off; he was checked but the ball went to Williams who managed to get over for a try converted by McCormick (8-0). The All Blacks, as the French experts had feared, were winning the ball almost all the time now, but there was a brief halt in their onslaughts when Muller was judged to have come through a line-out too quickly. Villepreux took the penalty kick and the ball went over off a post (8-3). This was the fastest Rugby of the tour—the fastest Rugby I can ever remember seeing. The All Blacks were determined to set the pace, but the natural quickness of the Frenchmen's reactions enabled them sometimes even to catch the New Zealanders napping. It was heady stuff.

After 23 minutes came another try made by Davis for Dick —exactly like the one they made between them against England at Twickenham. As before, the movement started with careful preparation at a line-out on the left near halfway. Jennings at No. 5 in the line-out pulled the ball down one-handed back towards the touchline where Meads caught it at No. 3. Meads held the ball momentarily to put the defence in doubt—then out came the ball through Going and Kirton to Cottrell. At this moment Davis, who had held back, suddenly accelerated and drifted inwards for a short pass from Cottrell. This inward swing took Davis past his man, whereupon he swung outwards again, straightened, drew the last defender, and gave Dick the ball and the try which McCormick converted (13-3).

The next bit of excitement came when Steel left the blind side and hurtled into the line on the open side. After this, the Frenchman sitting beside me with a comprehensive statistical chart on his knees announced that after 32 minutes' play the French had not yet won the ball from a single loose scrum, maul, or ruck. While he was trying vainly to explain this incomprehensible chart a violent din from the crowd announced that a penalty had been awarded against the French at a line-out. As McCormick ran up to take the kick at goal the din increased to a shattering pitch, and the kick failed. The All Blacks were not worried. Davis made an inside break and wove his way cleverly inwards to link with Gray. Then McCormick took Going's pass on the blind side of a set scrum. Lochore backed him up and Going ran round to the posts for a try which McCormick converted (18-3).

At halftime the supporters of the Static Game were looking a little smug. Clearly a solid pack and the kicking of Camberabero were the only means to stop these 'Black Devils'. The supporters of the Fluid Game were up in arms. How could the value of Gachassin possibly be judged fairly when he was given such a poor pack of forwards to work behind? To those of us who were uncommitted, it had been a wonderful first half of movement and attack worth coming many, many miles to see—one-sided, if you like, but that one side had played supremely well.

After the interval the occasion gained enormously in depth as the French suddenly forced their way into the game. Four minutes after the start of the second half Gachassin launched his threequarters from a line-out on the left near halfway; Lux, at outside centre, made a break, Capendeguy ran down the right wing and crosskicked. Storming up the middle, proving his fitness and speed came the tall Plantefol to gather the ball and to score a try near the posts for Villepreux to convert (18-8). More than that, four minutes later one of the French centres was obstructed in midfield, and Villepreux duly kicked a penalty goal (18-11). This was exciting stuff. For a moment Statics and Fluids in the crowd forgot their quarrel and combined in the singing of 'Allez La France'.

They combined too to make as much din as they could a few minutes later while McCormick was trying unsuccessfully to kick a penalty goal. They were not even hushed as their own Villepreux was only just wide (he got the length) with a penalty goal from inside the French half. McCormick now was successful with a penalty kick for an offence at a line-out (21-11), but two minutes later Villepreux replied in kind for an offence at a set scrum (21-14). The French forwards were now going much better than in the first half and they were making use of their native agility and quickness in the open.

Midway through this second half McCormick missed with yet another penalty kick at goal, and we had two further moves from the All Blacks' formidable repertoire. While Kirton ran to the left, Going passed direct to Cottrell on the right, and McCormick joined in as well. Then Lochore stood out of a scrum, sold a dummy towards Cottrell going to the blind side, and instead launched Kirton and the rest on the open side. The French were not tackling badly, and nothing came from these moves. Soon, however, Lochore sent Kirkpatrick charging away from the back of a line-out, Williams scored irresistibly, and McCormick converted (26-14). Five minutes later, Going ran on the open side of a set scrum and passed inside to Kirkpatrick who went over for another try (29-14). This was grand constructive play and, shortly before the end, the All Blacks heeled against the head at a set scrum, the French were caught offside, and McCormick's penalty kick took the score to 32-14.

This, we thought, was the end. But there was just time for the French backs to show their paces a second time. Launched by Gachassin, the threequarters went away at speed and Lux, again at outside centre, sold a dummy, turned inside, and ran on for a fine individual try made possible by some technically correct passing by the backs inside him. Villepreux converted. And the final score was a breathless 32-19.

It seemed unthinkable that any other match of the tour, Test or otherwise, could be as fast or contain such a wealth of attacking play, of thrust and counterthrust. Apart from the natural quickness of the French, where these opponents differed so much from those so far met by the All Blacks in Britain was in their mental outlook. The French were always alert for the slightest chance to be creative, even when they were many points behind. As for the native speed of the French, it was interesting to see such players as Kirton,

Cottrell—and even Going—at times overwhelmed by the pace at which things were happening. That the All Blacks managed to keep moving and to finish strongly at the end of a game played at this exceptional pace was a great credit to their basic fitness.

As at Bristol, Williams and Kirkpatrick played open and blind rather than right and left, and this seemed to suit them both. Certainly Kirkpatrick had played so convincingly in his last two games that the Test selectors clearly need have no qualms about picking him for the Test against France if they felt Tremain's form was not good enough. It was as I left the stadium after this match that the thought first came to me of how wonderfully well this All Black side would have fared on the dry grounds and in the sunshine of South Africa if they had been able, or willing, to go there.

For the moment, however, there was some more immediate business. The French national selectors had gone straight from the stadium to an elegant hotel in the neighbourhood, there to choose and to announce France's team for the Test the following Saturday. Some thirty-odd French journalists got into their Simcas, their Peugeots, and their Alfa Romeos and set off for the same hotel. The announcement of a French national side is an occasion in its own right. In England a team may be communicated to the press through an agency; in New Zealand the chairman of the Council may stand up and announce it at an after-match function or at a dinner. But in France the formalities have to be observed.

As we waited in groups in the foyer of the hotel, the discussion was serious and predictable. All were agreed that France must play both Plantefol and the 6 ft. 5 in. Dauga at lock so as to get the better of New Zealand in what was reckoned to be their one weak spot, the line-out. After that, opinions were sharply divided. The Statics said the obvious way to build on the expected French superiority at the line-out was to play Camberabero at stand-off so that he could keep feeding the French line-out forwards by kicking the ball back into touch. The Fluids said France could never hope to beat New Zealand by keeping play tight. Gachassin must be the stand-off half so that the ball could be moved about all over the place to break up the pattern and rhythm of All Black Rugby and to make the fullest use of French quickness and unpredictability.

Gachassin in truth had not had much chance to distinguish himself in the match we had just witnessed, but I hoped the choice would fall on him if only because his style of play seemed to me to represent the true traditions of French Rugby as I had known it and loved it and—for a season—tried to play it.

Led by the President of the French Rugby Federation, Monsieur Marcel Batigne, significantly (?) mopping his brow, the selectors presently filed one by one down the curved and lushly carpeted stairs leading from the first floor to the foyer. The last selector halted two or three stairs up to make the announcement. Dauga was in. Plantefol was in. And the stand-off half was . . . Gachassin.

Then came the barrage of questions from the scribbling journalists grouped round the foot of the stairs. 'Did you consider Camberabero?'—'Of course we did.' 'Is Spanghero really fit?'—'He will have to prove his fitness.' And so on. Until one journalist, noticing the absence of both Darrouy, who had captained France all the previous season and in South Africa, and of Fort, the previous season's pack-leader and captain in one Test in South Africa, innocently asked who the new captain was to be.

'Merde!' said the spokesman—which is not a very polite word to use in public—and we were given to understand that the selectors had forgotten to appoint a captain.

That is certainly what it looked like. And this impression was strengthened when they said they would announce the name of the captain before the team's training session in Paris the following Friday, the day before the Test. But some of the French journalists thought the selectors were being more subtle than that. 'They've chosen the captain, but they're afraid to tell us it's so-and-so', someone said. 'They don't want to spoil the good Press they'll get for just announcing Cachassin', said another. Whatever the reason, it did seem odd to British eyes that the French captain was to remain a mystery until the team assembled in Paris for the Test.

Expecting a Pushover

THE ALL BLACKS' team chosen to play against South-west France at Bayonne on Tuesday, November 21, was a strong one for a midweek match. This was largely because MacRae, Laidlaw, and Tremain had to prove their fitness and form after illness or injury. MacRae and Laidlaw were to play their first midweek game of the tour, and so was Dick. Wills was picked at No. 8 so that Kirkpatrick could have further match practice on the flank in case he was going to be needed to replace Tremain in this position. Altogether, this midweek side included eight of those who had played in the Test against Wales at Cardiff. This number was increased to nine when Thorne withdrew with a thigh injury and was replaced by Davis. This was, however—and it was to prove most significant—the first time on the tour that the forwards were to play without both Lochore and Meads. The side was to be captained for the first time by MacRae, with Tremain looking after the pack.

This side having been chosen and announced in Toulouse, the party left by bus for Bayonne along a road which gives magnificent views of the Pyrenees and their snow-capped peaks. A stop was made for sightseeing and lunch at Lourdes. Afterwards a brief visit was made to the Lourdes Rugby club where a match was in progress. Here indeed the All Blacks were able to watch in action four of their adversaries of the previous day, two of whom—Gachassin and Campaes—were due to play in the Test the following Saturday.

The All Blacks were to stay not at Bayonne but at Biarritz, the seaside resort a few miles away. Biarritz is a mixture of old and new, of ornate, rambling, down-at-heel villas and of modern blocks of flats. Its past is proclaimed by the *Avenue de la Reine Victoria* and the *Avenue Edouard VII*, but there is now a high-speed *Boulevard du General de Gaulle*. The municipal casino, beside a large sign saying 'Roulette', quaintly announced a *Festival Laurel et Hardy*.

The All Blacks stayed in a most modern hotel, well appointed and looking out over the beach and the sea. I chose one of the older establishments and found myself the only guest. In showing me to my room, Madame asked that I should not open one of the shutters because it had already twice fallen into the street many feet below and she had not the means to get it repaired. For many of these older buildings, which had lost their trade when the rich aristocrats and the royalty of Europe ceased to spend their winters in Biarritz, it seemed a toss-up whether they would decay and fall down before their turn came to be demolished to make way for a new block.

Just as you could meet a man in a bar who was not sure whether he was French or English, so Biarritz seemed still to cling to much of its past. It also seemed to manage to hold on to its summer weather much longer than most places: people were still to be seen surfing from the main beach.

It was a pity in a way that the All Blacks did not have longer in the relaxing atmosphere of Biarritz. They arrived on the Sunday evening and left again on the Wednesday. But this did mean that they were given a longer stay in Paris. While at Biarritz they also managed to make a short trip across the Spanish border to San Sebastian. It was in doing this that one of the party, having taken a photograph of one of the Spanish customs men, was made to surrender his film.

This was a little bit of excitement off the field of play, and there was more excitement when Stanley Couchman, who had been their liaison officer when they were in England, arrived in Biarritz loaded with mail from London for them. Stanley, now a member of the Rugby Football Union Committee, had been liaison officer for the Wallabies the previous season and had in his playing days been to South Africa with the 1938 Lions.

The opposition at Bayonne for the All Blacks was reckoned by the French Press to be by far the weakest of the French sides. The South-west in fact included only one man, Sitjar, the wing forward and captain, who had played in a Test against any of the home countries. He had been in and out of the French national side since he was first capped in 1964.

Apart from Sitjar, the best known of the French players was Dehez, the full-back. Dehez had been top scorer, with 52 points, on the recent French tour of South Africa, where he had played in the second Test as a stand-off half. His points there had been made up of six dropped goals, five conversions, and eight penalty goals. Crampagne, the South-west's left wing, and Esponda and Lasserre, the props, had also been to South Africa. Lasserre, oddly enough, had played in one of the South African Tests at No. 8.

Otherwise the local side was composed of players who had yet to make a name for themselves. Latanne, for instance, was a regular member of his club's second team, not because of any trouble over a licence but because his club thought they had two better wings than Latanne. The two halfbacks' only claim to attention was when they had played together for the Joinville Battalion. Joinville is near Paris, and it is there that many of France's best sportsmen have found themselves posted for their period of national service. It is interesting indeed to note the large number of recent French Test players whose selection has seemed to owe a great deal to the progress they have made while at the Joinville Battalion.

It was not then a side of much reputation that faced the All Blacks at Bayonne. Indeed, we had been led to expect it to be the weakest opposition the All Blacks would be up against on the whole of the tour. Since the All Blacks were fielding nine of the Test team that had played against Wales, I expected an easy victory.

MATCH NINE

v. SOUTH-WEST FRANCE
AT BAYONNE
TUESDAY, NOVEMBER 21, 1967

South-West France

J. L. Dehez (Agen)

J. P. Latanne (Lourdes), C. Goumandie (Perigueux), M. Marot (Brive), J. Crampagne (Begles)

H. Magois (La Rochelle), J. Fourow (Cognac)

B. Dutin (Mont-de-Marsan), M. Sitjar (Agen), capt., J. Laplace (Biarritz), J. Foulquier (Carcassonne), P. Darbos (Dax), M. Lasserre (Agen), N. Dargeles (Tarbes), J. Esponda (Perpignan)

All Blacks

G. F. Kember

M. J. Dick, W. L. Davis, W. M. Birtwistle

I. R. MacRae, capt., M. A. Herewini

C. R. Laidlaw

M. C. Wills, K. R. Tremain, S. C. Strahan, A. G. Jennings, I. A. Kirkpatrick, K. F. Gray, B. E. McLeod, A. E. Hopkinson

REFEREE: P. E. DICKINSON (Wales)

SOUTH-WEST FRANCE 14 POINTS

Try—Latanne; 3 penalty goals—Dehez; conversion —Dehez

ALL BLACKS 18 POINTS

3 tries—Kirkpatrick, Dick, Tremain; 3 penalty goals—Kember

Shocks for the All Blacks

As WE MADE our way to the ground, everything seemed ready for an exhibition of fluent Rugby by the All Blacks. The clouds were thin and high, and blue sky could be seen between them. High above the cramped and jumbled russet roofs of the old town were the two slim, light-grey spires of Bayonne cathedral. Down below, swarming up the hill from the banks of the easy-moving Adour River, were thousands of Basques in their black berets. This corner of France is a great stronghold of Rugby and well known for its addiction to the open game. What these people wanted to see was a display of attacking football such as the All Blacks had given at Toulouse. I doubt if any of them imagined for a moment that the local side would make a real match of it.

The fact that the All Blacks were penalised at the first lineout—and that Dehez duly kicked a penalty goal—probably did not alter the crowd's anticipation. They still gave generous applause to the All Blacks' first movement. The ball came rapidly along the line to Birtwistle on the left, MacRae took an inside pass, the forwards piled in, and the ball went speeding back towards the right. But it was not long before the spectators began to realise that the All Blacks this day were eminently fallible. The All Blacks offended at another line-out and Dehez only just missed with the long and difficult penalty kick. Then Sitjar broke away from a line-out and set his side an aggressive example by selling a highly convincing dummy to the All Blacks' defence.

There was soon the most unusual sight—almost unique so far on the tour—of the All Blacks winning initial possession at a line-out, holding the ball, but then having it taken off them before they could do anything with it. Then the French got the ball cleanly from a New Zealand throw-in at a line-out. And the next time the All Blacks got the ball, Herewini threw it over MacRae's shoulder. It was indeed rather against the run of play that Kember kicked a penalty goal after 19 minutes, the French stand-off half having been caught standing offside at a line-out (3-3).

The French were soon back on the attack. Their stand-off kicked deep diagonally, and Kember had to scramble the ball into touch. The French lobbed the throw-in over the back of the line-out. But they seemed to have lost their chance when the referee was not satisfied with the throw and ordered a set scrum with the All Blacks to put in. The All Blacks were not sound in this match, however. They got the ball back from this scrum all right, but Herewini dropped Laidlaw's pass, MacRae fumbled his attempted pick-up, and an All Black flykicked the ball straight into the hands of Latanne—who gratefully touched down for a try which Dehez converted with a fine kick (8-3 to the French).

Kember soon reduced the arrears with a penalty goal and was only just short with another long penalty kick at goal. But the drop-out after this second kick was taken by Crampagne who put the ball well down inside the New Zealand 25 with a mighty kick. Before the All Blacks could escape they were penalised yet again at a line-out, and Dehez kicked his second penalty goal (11-6 to the French).

By now, of course, chauvinism had taken possession of the crowd. As Foulquier lay injured on the ground after a ruck, they hurled their shrillest abuse at the All Blacks. Foulquier was not badly hurt, but the crowd turned their indignant wrath on to the referee when he had the nerve to signal a penalty to the All Blacks for something that had happened at that same maul. Kember failed with this kick at goal. But a minute later Gray peeled from a line-out on the right, Herewini kicked towards the left corner, and Kirkpatrick followed up for a try (11-9 to the French).

There was not long to go now to halftime, but what time there was was taken up mainly with French attacks. Sitjar showed his quality by breaking quickly from the blind-side flank to the open side of a set scrum and there taking his scrum-half's pass, sidestepping Herewini, and running through. Then a fine leap and catch by Laplace at a line-out began a bout of effervescent French passing. Just before the interval, moreover, Dehez came up close to a line-out and only just failed with a most ambitious dropkick at goal. So it was 11-9 to the French at halftime, the first time the All Blacks had been behind at the interval in any match of the tour.

It was already clear that the All Blacks badly missed the strength and drive of Meads and Lochore in the rucks. In their absence there seemed to be no-one capable of making a thrust close to the pack and at the same time no-one capable of robbing a Frenchman of the ball. Tactically, too, the All Blacks seemed unimaginative, almost timid. Laidlaw was playing well enough, but Herewini was having one of those days when he repeatedly turned in his tracks and banged the ball back into touch. MacRae, also, was doing a lot of kicking —though his kicks were usually of a more constructive kind.

The French went straight back on to the attack at the start of the second half, and their stand-off half only just missed with a dropkick at goal following a line-out. Next, Tremain queried the referee's decision to penalise him for coming round a set scrum too early, and the referee ordered the All Blacks to retire a further ten yards. Then, when Laidlaw had been overwhelmed behind his own line following a line-out, Dutin missed a chance of a French try by fumbling his pick-up from the subsequent set scrum. The French pressure continued, with Sitjar taking a tap-down at the back of a line-out and crashing into Herewini's tackle, thus setting up a loose ball for his forwards to exploit beyond the advantage line. This was exciting to watch. The only sad point was that Here-wini was injured in tackling Sitjar. He did not go off the field, but he was far from comfortable thereafter.

An up-and-under penalty punt by Laidlaw switched the initiative back to the All Blacks for a while. When the French were penalised for incorrect peeling from a line-out, Kember took a long kick at goal. An inside break by MacRae had the French scampering across the field to cover Dick, and this pressure was soon rewarded with three points. First, however, Kember made such a poor attempt to kick a penalty goal from quite a simple position that I wondered if he deliberately aimed to let the ball fall short, hoping for five points instead of three. The ball fell short and to the left of the posts. The All Blacks got possession and switched it out towards the right. After Davis had run, Dick was put over near the right corner (12-11 to the All Blacks).

The French reacted furiously to the loss of their lead, and in three minutes they had got it back again. First their scrum half made a break close to a set scrum and Sitjar supported him. Then one of the New Zealand backs was caught standing offside while a line-out was taking place, and Dehez kicked his third penalty goal (14-12 to the French). At this point there were 28 minutes to go, and the French were playing with such confidence and passing so correctly that I began to feel they could win. It was notable that when Laidlaw tried to run through the back of a line-out he was blocked and well and truly dumped, and that when Jennings took a tap-down and tried to run round the back of a line-out in the manner of a Meads, he was not only blocked but knocked backwards by the force of an immediate double tackle by two determined Frenchmen.

For seventeen hectic and noisy minutes the French went on playing with determination and confidence, and it was difficult to see how the All Blacks could score against them. The French survived a brief period during which Dutin was off the field having a cut head bandaged. They also survived a fairly simple penalty kick at goal by Kember when one of their centres had been caught standing offside at a line-out. In their keenness, however, one of them got in front of the kicker at a drop-out, thus causing a set scrum, with the All Blacks to put in, at the middle of the 25. The French scrum-half came round too quickly on to Laidlaw—and this was a penalty kick Kember was not going to miss (15-14 to the All Blacks).

The indignant fury of the volatile crowd was comic to behold: how could any competent referee award a penalty in front of the posts at this stage of a game? Such a crowd thinks only of the referee on these occasions. No thought is given to the possibility that the offender may have done something rather stupid.

The All Blacks had not been run so close since their match against West Wales at Swansea. Now there were just eleven minutes to go and, as at Swansea, the All Blacks scored a late try. Herewini sent up a Garryowen, the forwards piled in, and Tremain scored (18-14). Herewini failed with the conversion kick, the final whistle blew, and the touchjudges and the local police took the wise—and in this part of the world not unusual —precaution of escorting the referee from the paddock.

There were plenty of excuses for the All Blacks' generally disappointing performance. Davis, suffering from leg trouble, was not fully fit before the match started. An X-ray later revealed that Herewini's injury was a cracked vertebra, and he was advised not to play again for four weeks—which meant not until after the end of the tour. Kember had been successful with only three of ten kicks at goal. The referee, like Mr d'Arcy at Leicester and Mr Gwynne Walters at Bristol, had been very strict at the line-out. But what really mattered most, I felt, was the absence of Meads and Lochore. They were not there to provide impetus to the forward play and therefore to the side as a whole. And they were not there to provide a hard core to the rucks, so as to prevent their opponents from getting the ball back.

The French indeed won much more of the ball in the loose than had any other side on the tour against the All Blacks. The French were also quick and alert in making and seizing chances to be creative. They were never content, as some British sides seemed to be, merely to avoid defeat by a big score. The French themselves wanted to attack and to score tries. Watching from the stand, Gachassin, who was to play at stand-off half against the All Blacks in the Test the following Saturday, must have been delighted to note the relative success of the relentlessly creative methods of the South-west team.

After the match there was a reception in a pelota court at the Bayonne club. The club was originally a rowing club— hence its name, Aviron Bayonnais—but it now caters for many different sports. It was founded in 1904 and numbers among its heroes one Owen Roe, a Welshman of course, who started the club on its tradition of open football. The greatest exponent of this type of game that the club has produced is Jean Dauger who, as almost any Frenchman will tell you, was the greatest centre France has ever had. He played only once for France, against Scotland in 1953, because someone then discovered he had played as a Rugby League Test player at the age of seventeen.

It was at a bar run by Dauger that, later the same evening, I came across some of the French players who had been on their country's tour of New Zealand in 1961. André and Guy Boniface, the centres, were there, and André said that if he was younger he would pack his bags and take his family off to New Zealand. He would like to play behind a New Zealand pack of forwards in the style of play Charlie Saxton and Fred Allen were demanding. Albaladejo, the stand-off half, said that what struck him most about New Zealand was the silence as he prepared to kick at goal. He said it put him off much more than the jeers and boos he was used to at home. Michel Celaya, who played at No. 8, lock, and wing forward for France in a career spanning nine seasons, was also there. He was now coach to the Biarritz club nearby. I was especially pleased to meet him, since he had been captain of Biarritz club during the season I had played with them there about eleven or twelve years before.

The Big Surprise

THAT SAME TUESDAY evening the All Blacks' selectors, Saxton, Allen, Lochore, and MacRae, sat down in their hotel at Biarritz and picked their team for the Test at Colombes in Paris the following Saturday. They made three changes from the side which had beaten Wales 13-6 two weeks before. Going came in at halfback in place of Laidlaw, Kirkpatrick was chosen for his first Test on the flank at the expense of Tremain, and Steel was preferred to Birtwistle on the left wing. Laidlaw, Tremain, and Birtwistle had all been injured recently, but all three were officially considered fit for selection for the Test.

The big surprise was the dropping of Laidlaw. He had played wonderfully well in the mud and rain of the Cardiff Test, and his intimate mutual understanding with Kirton had counted for a great deal in that match. He had not played between the Cardiff Test and the Bayonne match, but I thought he had played well enough at Bayonne to be sure of his place for Colombes. It was at Colombes that he had played his first Test, in 1964 with Herewini as his first five-eighth.

Going, of course, had been having a splendid tour, scoring try after try and making others. Nobody begrudged him his chance in what was to be his second Test, his first having been against Australia the previous August. He was a constant worrier of opposing defences with his restless probing and running on the fringes of scrums and rucks. Against this had to be set a pass shorter and less accurate than Laidlaw's and also the fact that he had not the close understanding with Kirton that Laidlaw had. That is not say that Going and Kirton had not been combining well. They had played together at Manchester, Bristol, and Toulouse and had hit it off remarkably well for a relatively scratch pair. But, inevitably, their degree of co-operation could not equal that of Laidlaw and Kirton who had been regularly playing together for several years. Perhaps the British attach more importance to a pairing at scrum-half and stand-off half than New Zealanders do to that between halfback and first five-eighth. To me the angle and timing of the run of the stand-off half, and especially the exact point at which he must receive the ball if a constructive three-quarter movement is to take place, can only be achieved through repeated practice and playing with the same scrum half.

Tremain, whose play must have been affected by his Achilles tendon trouble, had not been showing his old zest and thrust. He had already played 33 times for New Zealand—more times than anyone else except Colin Meads—but it was no great surprise to find him now displaced by Kirkpatrick, who so far on tour had played four games on the flank and only one at No. 8. Kirkpatrick had increasingly shown drive and pace, especially in supporting the work of Going who had been the halfback in four of Kirkpatrick's five tour games (the one exception was Bayonne). Kirkpatrick had not the experience to give Lochore the same support that Tremain had done at the line-out. And he would not be as effective at the rucks, thus leaving even more work to be done here by Meads and Lochore. But, especially from an attacking point of view, the choice of Kirkpatrick seemed fully justified.

There had never been much to choose between Steel and Birtwistle for the left wing. Steel was the more forceful player and the one more likely to be effective in leaving the blind side and coming into the line as an extra man on the open side. But Birtwistle was the more cultured footballer with much more reliable hands and greater subtlety in his running. The choice of one in preference to the other was not likely to rouse strong passions, except perhaps in Canterbury or the Waikato.

The morning after the Bayonne match was beautifully sunny and warm in Biarritz, where the All Blacks were due to train before flying later in the day to Paris. It was a great tonic after so much rain and cloud in Britain, and at Lyons too, to breathe the gentle air of the South of France and to feel again the warmth of a clear sun. After a few turns round the paddock, Allen ushered his players up into a corner of one of the uncovered stands in the sunshine where Saxton and he could talk to them.

I imagine this was an important 20-minute period in relation to the tour as a whole. Travel weariness, change of temperature, change of diet, controversial selections and nagging, though minor, injuries all presented possible problems at this stage. Even allowing for all the excuses, the All Blacks had not played well the day before at Bayonne. Here was a combination of circumstances which might have upset a lesser team with lesser leaders. There must have been plenty to talk about as they sat in the Biarritz sun.

Predictably, this little session was followed by one of Fred Allen's most blistering practices. 'Now! Now! Now!' he spat out as the forwards hurtled up the paddock interpassing and backing up in formation; and 'Spin! Spin! Spin! Spin!' and 'Straighten up! Straighten up! Straighten up!' as the ball sped crisply out to the wing. It was exhausting stuff in the heat, and at the end of it there were no soft drinks and no French liaison officer in sight. Luckily Stanley Couchman, his duties as postman completed, had stayed on with the party. With his unfailing keenness, he now set about procuring drinks. The results of his labours have seldom been so heartily appreciated. Thus did the All Blacks prepare for Paris.

The French, as is their custom nowadays, were due to assemble in Paris on the Thursday, to train in Paris on the Friday morning, and then to go off to a hotel outside the city for peace and quiet that evening and night. As they had said they would, the French selectors officially announced the name of their captain on the Friday morning. The job was given to Christian Carrère who, at 24, was far from being the senior member of the side in terms either of age or experience. He had previously played for France for only one season and he had had little or no experience of leadership. He had played against the All Blacks as a wing forward at Lyons under the captaincy of Herrero, who was his club captain at Toulon.

Many people in France seemed to wish that Herrero had been included in the team instead of Spanghero at No. 8. Spanghero, to start with, had recently broken a rib cartilage and was therefore not entirely fit. It was also pointed out firstly that Herrero was a more accomplished No. 8 (Spanghero having usually played at lock for France) and secondly that Herrero had the height to stand up to Lochore at the back of the line-out. Herrero had much experience, having played against New Zealand in Paris in 1964 and having been a more or less regular member of the side ever since. But he had not been able to go on the recent French tour of South Africa.

This question of whether or not players who went to South Africa should have priority over those who could not make themselves available for that tour was another controversy which added to the noise in the bars and cafés of Southern France. In the event, the chosen side included only four who did not go to South Africa. These were Gruarin, indisputably France's best tight head prop; the controversial little Gachassin at stand-off half; and Capendeguy and Campaes, the two wing threequarters, who were really standing in for players injured or hopelessly out of form. The team also included only five who had not played in one of the three games the All Blacks had just played in France. These five were Cabanier, France's regular hooker since 1964; Abadie, a 33-year-old prop who had just recently won his first cap in South Africa at loose head; the 6 ft. 5 in. Dauga, who had been a regular in the side, either at lock or No. 8, since before playing against New Zealand in 1964; Puget, a tough little scrum-half who had been injured while playing for South-west France against the 1963–64 All Blacks at Bordeaux and who had not played against any of the home countries until 1966; and Dourthe, a young centre who had played for France the previous season while still a schoolboy. In fact Dourthe had played against Rumania at the end of November, 1966, when his age was 18 years and seven days, thus becoming the youngest French player ever to take part in a Test. He went on to play against all the home countries and Australia and then to tour South Africa.

Spanghero had become the toast of France in 1964 after being chosen at the last minute for France's tour of South Africa that year and astonishing South Africans with his strength, his thrust, and his youthful fitness. He is an awkward man to fit into a pack, being just lacking in inches for the line-out work expected of a Test lock or No. 8 and lacking the agility needed on the flank. On the 1967 French tour of South Africa he had been used as a flanker in a Test, but it is possible that his final position will be prop. Quilis, the wing forward who had played against the All Blacks at Toulouse, had first played for France on the recent tour of South Africa . . . as a wing threequarter.

The French practice on the Friday morning was directed by Jean Prat who had captained France against Bob Stuart's All Blacks in 1954 and scored the try by which France won 3-0. Between 1947 and 1955, Jean Prat missed only one French Test (against Ireland in 1951 because of illness) and now he had become the regular coach to the national team. He had also been a highly successful coach to the French team in South Africa in 1964, being the ideal complement to the strict managership of Serge Saulnier. The most notable feature of this practice this Friday morning was that the tall Plantefol was stationed not at No. 5 in the line-out but further back, presumably to mark Lochore.

On the eve of the Test it seemed that France had just a slight chance of success. The All Blacks' three games in France had shown that the high standard of French forward technique (derived probably from uniformity of coaching) and the natural quick reactions of the French could unsettle the rhythm and pattern of the All Blacks' play. The problem for France was how to impose their native qualities.

Apart from using such occasions as drop-outs and tapped penalties as often as possible for running in a broken field, the French could have some hope of getting a lot of the ball at the line-outs. Dauga possessed a combination of height, jumping skill, and experience which put him above any New Zealand line-out expert. Plantefol was not far behind him in jumping skill and height and had recently done well in Tests in South Africa—no mean passport to success at Colombes. They promised to be a rare handful for Strahan and Meads. As we were jostled and breathed upon in the packed, lurching electric train from the Gare St Lazare to Colombes, we were not to know that the French would deploy their considerable line-out strength with such rigid lack of imagination.

MATCH TEN

v FRANCE
AT COLOMBES
SATURDAY, NOVEMBER 25, 1967

France

P. *Villepreux (Toulouse)*

J. M. *Capendeguy (Begles), C. Dourthe (Dax),*
M. *Trillo (Begles), A. Campaes (Lourdes)*

J. *Gachassin (Lourdes), M. Puget (Brive)*

W. *Spanghero (Narbonne), C. Carrere (Toulon),*
capt., A. Plantefol (Agen), B. Dauga (Mont-de-
Marsan), A. Quilis (Narbonne), A. Abadie
(Graulhet), J. M. Cabanier (Montauban), A.
Gruarin (Toulon)

New Zealand

W. F. *McCormick*

M. J. *Dick, W. L. Davis, A. G. Steel*

I. R. *MacRae, E. W. Kirton*

S. M. *Going*

B. J. *Lochore, capt., G. C. Williams, S. C.*
Strahan, C. E. Meads, I. A. Kirkpatrick, K. F.
Gray, B. E. McLeod, B. L. Muller

REFEREE: R. P. BURRELL (Scotland)

FRANCE 15 POINTS

**Try—Campaes; dropped goal—Gachassin; 3 penalty
goals—Villepreux**

NEW ZEALAND 21 POINTS

**4 tries—Going, Steel, Kirkpatrick, Dick; 3 conver-
sions—McCormick; Penalty goal—McCormick**

The 'Hardest' Test

IT WAS a grey, misty afternoon as the two teams stood still for the national anthems. While the anthems were being played I counted 30 photographers busily moving from player to player, seizing their chance to get head and shoulders portraits while the players for once were still. This always forms part of the prelude to Tests at Colombes nowadays, and it seems to me to be an undignified, disrespectful, and crude procedure.

The French kicked off, the referee ordered a scrum back with New Zealand to put in, the All Blacks were penalised, and Villepreux was given his first kick at goal before the game had got properly under way. The French, with the tall Plantefol stationed at No. 7, threw in long to the first line-out. Gruarin took the tap-down, Spanghero carried on and kicked, and New Zealand had to touch down for a 25. As soon as the French were forced back into their own half it was noticeable that they were already taking Quilis out of the line-outs to become an additional defender against New Zealand's expected thrusts in midfield.

The first points, after four minutes, came more tamely than that. Carrère was penalised for an offence at a loose scrum, and McCormick kicked a straightforward penalty goal. It was just after this Kirkpatrick fell awkwardly in making a tackle on Campaes and broke his nose. He did not go off. After a brief delay France won a good heel at a set scrum on the left, Gachassin swung his threequarters into action, Villepreux came dashing into the line outside the centres, and his grubkick led to a line-out on the right inside the New Zealand 25. The French won the ball from this line-out. Gachassin took a quick drop at goal, and the ball, seemingly ages in the air, just dropped over the bar, making the score 3-3 after eight minutes. It was a promising start for the crowd of some 45,000.

Their hearts must have been in their mouths a minute or

two later, however, when from a set scrum on the right near the French line Going's pass missed out Kirton. MacRae took it and passed to Davis, and Davis slipped past his man. He had Steel unmarked outside him but chose to try to dummy his way inside. Villepreux tore into him with a superb head-on tackle, the ball was thrown forward by the impact—and the danger for France was averted. They also survived another penalty kick at goal by McCormick and a formidable charge by Meads.

It was while he was on the ground after making this charge that Meads's scalp was ripped open by a French boot, an injury which clearly caused great pain and later required three stitches. This was one of a number of incidents of foul play by each side, thoroughly justifying the adjectives 'brutal' and 'savage' used by spectators at the end of the game. A few minutes after Meads's injury Villepreux fell on the ball bravely, following an up-and-under kick by Going, and emerged with two ribs broken. Clearly it was going to be a hard, hard battle.

After 24 minutes Going made a mark, and his subsequent dropkick at goal was just short. Two minutes later, however, the irrepressible little man scored a try. The French heeled from a set scrum near their left corner. Carrère, on the blind side, picked the ball up but let it go wildly. Meads and Kirkpatrick made off with it: Going went with them and scored, too far out for McCormick to convert (6-3). This time it took the French little more than a minute to equalise, a New Zealander being penalised at a loose scrum, and Villepreux kicking a long penalty goal (6-6).

Villepreux had another (unaccepted) chance to kick a penalty goal just after this when McCormick, running with the ball, was penalised for handing off with his forearm instead of an open palm. Soon afterwards, Cabanier was too early in leaving the front of a line-out to harass Going, and McCormick failed with the subsequent penalty kick at goal. Next the French posted Gruarin, a prop forward, at scrum-half at a line-out and got Puget to act as stand-off half, giving them an extra back; but one of the backs knocked on. Then Gachassin was wide with another dropkick at goal.

After 40 minutes, however, there came yet another of the MacRae-Davis closes. The movement for this one began from a set scrum on the right. Davis, as usual, first hung back and then accelerated inwards for his short pass from MacRae. This time Davis could not quite get clear of clinging French arms, but MacRae moved swiftly round outside him, took his pass, and put Steel over. McCormick converted from near the left touchline (11-6). By the watch it should have been half-time now, but the referee added seven minutes to the first half for stoppages.

They were eventful minutes too. First we saw a purple patch of New Zealand attacking rhythm. They whipped the ball crisply out all along the line to the left wing where Steel could not beat his man. No matter: All Black support play ensured that possession was retained. Going broke ahead and, when his progress was checked, the ball was sent back across the paddock to the right with McCormick now joining in the attack. This led to a line-out on the right with Dick poised to come into the line between Kirton and MacRae. Instead, Kirton kicked diagonally left, Dick hurtled after the ball, and probably only his knock-on prevented a try. Again New Zealand attacked, and this time McCormick came up for an inside pass from MacRae. After all this splendid attacking play by the All Blacks it came as something of an anti-climax when, a moment or two before halftime, Muller was penalised for a late tackle on Puget, and Villepreux kicked his second penalty goal from a long way out (11-9 to New Zealand).

The photographers now swarmed back on to the paddock to take their close-ups of bloody noses and bleeding heads. This time I counted between 30 and 40 non-combatants of various descriptions milling around the players in midfield. The players, of course, were in conference, but French discussions were to produce no improvement in their positional play at the line-out in the second half. It was a sensible idea to put the tall Plantefol to mark Lochore at No. 7, but silly to leave Strahan at No. 5 marked by no one taller than Spanghero.

The French arrangement on their own throw-in was utterly incomprehensible. For this their players stayed in the same positions. Their wings almost invariably threw either to No. 5, where Spanghero was outclassed by Strahan, or to the back where Lochore was not going to be outdone by a stripling like Plantefol. The French wings almost totally ignored Dauga, at No. 3, who was their best jumper. The obvious arrangement on a French throw-in would have been to have Dauga at No. 5, where he would have had a good chance of beating Strahan, and Plantefol at No. 3, where he would at least have jumped higher than Meads—that is if the wings could be persuaded to throw the ball intelligently. Of course, as the anti-Spanghero group was quick to point out, what was really wanted was the tall Herrero in the side in place of Spanghero. The French were still in the match all right, but with more sensible deployment of their men at the line-outs they could have got much more of the ball for themselves and also made life much harder for the All Blacks. It seemed such a waste.

The first incident of the second half was a late tackle of Kirton by Plantefol, for which McCormick failed with a difficult penalty kick at goal. Next Kirton ran on the blind side and worked a scissors with Dick. Then MacRae made an inside break but passed the ball forward. Now the French fullback, taking a leaf out of McCormick's book, ran on the blind side from his scrum-half's pass and gave a run down the wing to Campaes who crosskicked. Spanghero, gathering the crosskick, knocked on, but New Zealand were penalised for injuring one of the French props during the subsequent set scrum. Villepreux kicked his third penalty goal, making it 12-11 to France with 10 minutes of the second half gone.

For fourteen minutes the French held on to this lead. They were hectic and dangerous minutes for both teams. Lochore did his ploy of standing out of a scrum and taking a pass from his halfback. This time, instead of passing either to Kirton on one side of him or to MacRae on the other, he sold a dummy and charged off towards the French line himself. Then he picked the ball up at a set scrum and threw it out to MacRae, whose drop at goal was touched in flight. Kirton came into the line a second time. Another New Zealand attack broke down, and the French took the ball away at their feet. Fists flew at a maul, and steam could be seen rising from the next set scrum. The French shovelled the ball out along the line to Campaes

6—TAB

who crosskicked dangerously, but Lochore got back and made a mark. Meads peeled from a line-out, MacRae carried on, was tackled, and Meads was there to push onwards again. McCormick made an unsuccessful attempt to kick a long penalty goal when Dauga was offside. McCormick made one of his dummy entries into the line and Dick had a run. The French were now pulling Quilis out of set scrums as well as line-outs to strengthen their defence in midfield. They were defending with great ingenuity.

After fourteen minutes of this, however, they relaxed for one moment their vigilance at a maul following a line-out. Going saw his chance of a break, Meads and Kirkpatrick went with him and Kirkpatrick scored a try which McCormick converted (16-12 to New Zealand). Now the pressure was really on. Kirton ran on the blind side and McCormick nipped round with him. This was checked, and then Dick came tearing into the line outside Kirton. Eventually, four minutes after Kirkpatrick's try, the pressure told again. The ball went loose after an attacking run by McCormick, the French did not deal with it firmly, and Dick, together with Williams, touched it down over the French line for a try converted by McCormick. This was a grand surge of power and pressure by the All Blacks. Ten points in less than five minutes had taken them from 11-12 to 21-12. Although there were still fourteen minutes to go, the match was to all intents and purposes won and lost.

It was not the end of the game however: twice the French were to run cleverly from tapped penalties. The first time they could not complete their move. The second time Puget ran up the right touchline, Quilis carried on turning inside, and little Gachassin sprinted away towards the New Zealand posts before sending out a long, high pass leftwards to Campaes who scored near the left-hand corner. I thought the last pass was forward, but in the last moments of a match in which the issue is already settled I would not blame a referee for turning a blind eye and allowing such beautiful running to come to its natural fruition.

The errors of the French in their line-out positional play had denied us the pleasure of seeing Gachassin repeatedly sending his threequarters into action, but these last two movements had given a hint of what might have been. They were a reminder that when Gachassin was first chosen at stand-off half instead of wing threequarter—this was for France's match against Wales at Colombes in March 1965—the French scored 19 points in the first half.

I thought Kirkpatrick had fully justified his inclusion on the flank in preference to Tremain. Steel, to give him his due, had taken his one scoring pass impeccably. Going, predictably, had done a great deal of valuable probing and nosing but had not been able to give Kirton the passes that Laidlaw could have been expected to provide. Here it was a question of two contrasting styles of play. MacRae at last was in something like his best form, and Strahan had begun to look like a mature player.

Brian Lochore said at the dinner afterwards that this was the hardest Test he had ever played in. He was not referring just to the roughness and the toughness, as he made clear when he went on to comment on the great rise in the standard of French play generally since he had last been in France, with the 1963–64 All Blacks.

An interesting outside opinion was voiced by Dr Louis Babrow, who had toured New Zealand with the 1937 Springboks and was now chairman of the Western Province selection committee. He had travelled to Paris to see the match, having seen it written that the 1967 All Blacks were as good a side as the 1937 Springboks—whom many people have regarded as the best Rugby team of all time. Dr Babrow said after this match at Colombes that the 1967 All Blacks were *better* than the 1937 Springboks. They certainly went down well in France where their methodical play and the excellence of their technique appealed to the realists. In their four matches in France they had scored 87 points to 51. They had scored sixteen tries to four. They had played some magnificent Rugby. France last saw them standing and sitting in a relaxed group at a bar at Le Bourget airport, singing to Nathan's accompaniment. Then they got into their plane to fly to Edinburgh via London airport....

An Unusual Fifteen

WHILE THE All Blacks were in Edinburgh the official announcement was made that their two matches in Ireland, against an Irish Combined Fifteen in Belfast on December 13 and against Ireland in Dublin on December 16, had been cancelled because of an epidemic of foot and mouth disease in England. This was a very severe outbreak of the disease, and the Irish were trying to keep it from spreading into their country. At the time they were already talking of closing their ports and airports, and an official request had been made by the Irish Government asking Irish people living in England not to make the traditional journey home to Ireland for Christmas.

Instead of these two matches it was agreed that a match should be played against the Barbarians at Twickenham on December 16. No substitute game was arranged for December 13. Charlie Saxton summed up the feelings of the party: 'We are all very disappointed that we are unable to visit and play in Northern Ireland and the Republic of Ireland but, as an alternative, we will be thrilled to play the Barbarians, especially at Twickenham. To most New Zealanders, Twickenham is the home of Rugby Football, and it will also give us the opportunity to see a little more of London'.

A match between the Barbarians and the touring side of the season had become traditional in Britain since the first such match arranged at the last minute for the Wallabies of 1947–48. But, because this 1967 tour was so short, room had not been found for the fixture when the itinerary was being drawn up. All previous matches between the Barbarians and touring sides had been held at Cardiff. The last time a Test in the British Isles had been interfered with by disease was in March, 1962, when the Ireland-Wales match was postponed to the following season because of an outbreak of smallpox in South Wales.

The immediate business, however, was the match against Scottish Districts at Melrose the Wednesday after the French Test. The party stayed in Edinburgh the whole week, since the journey to Melrose could easily be made by bus on the day of the game. The one real problem for the All Blacks' selectors for this Melrose match was whom to have at first five-eighth now that Kirton needed a rest and Herewini had been told not to play again on the tour. It was decided to have Cottrell at first five-eighth and Kember at second five-eighth, with McCormick playing again at full-back. Up to now Cottrell had played exclusively on tour at second five-eighth and Kember at full-back.

Nathan was at last declared fit to resume playing after breaking his jaw at Leicester on October 28, four and a half weeks earlier. He had missed a possible eight matches. He and Tremain were to be the flankers at Melrose, and both of them probably had high hopes of playing their way into the Test team against Scotland at Murrayfield the following Saturday. Laidlaw was another with hopes of playing in the Test. He had lost his Test piece to Going and was now to play his second midweek match of the tour. Lochore decided to play at lock for the first time on the tour, with Smith as his partner. With Cottrell and Kember at first and second five-eighth, Lochore at lock, and Nathan back in the side, it was thus an unusual-looking fifteen the All Blacks had chosen for Melrose.

Normally, on a full-length tour, a visiting team in the Melrose-Hawick area can expect to meet a homogeneous side representing the tough school of Scottish Rugby, the Border country. This is the home of Jim Telfer, Frank Laidlaw, and Derrick Grant, of the last Lions tour, and also of H. F. McLeod of the 1959 Lions. But since the 1967 All Blacks were to play only two games in Scotland, the opposition on this occasion was really Scotland's second fifteen. Technically and individually this should be a better side than a side representing the Borders or South of Scotland, but it would not have the pride or the understanding of a team drawn exclusively from the smaller area. A similar side to this 1967 one had beaten the 1965 Springboks, it is true, but those Springboks, who came to Ireland and Scotland shortly before the

1965 Springbok tour of New Zealand, did not win any of the five matches of their short tour. No one, I think, expected much from this Scottish Districts side.

This feeling was only increased by the knowledge that the Districts team was more or less the side which, as the junior fifteen, had been beaten 26-8 in the Scottish trial the previous Saturday. What had happened was that the senior side of that trial had, with one exception, been named as the Scotland fifteen for the Test the following Saturday, and the junior fifteen, slightly altered, had been chosen as the District team for this midweek match.

Even so the side, as originally selected, included six Test players, Blaikie at full-back, Whyte on the wing, Welsh in the centre, Simmers at stand-off half, Suddon at prop, and Hunter at lock. Whyte, however, who had recently had a hip operation, withdrew because of a bang on the knee, and Suddon dropped out at the last minute with flu. There was a New Zealander in the team, too, T. K. McDonald at prop. And Simmers, who was to captain the team, had played Rugby in New Zealand. The cosmopolitan nature of the side could be seen by looking at the clubs represented—the Wasps and Guy's Hospital, of London, for instance, as well as London Scottish.

This Districts side had not trained together at all as a squad like the Welsh teams, but the Scots did hope to get a fair amount of the ball from their tall line-out men, Hunter, McHarg, and Arneil. Hunter, now over thirty, had played against New Zealand in 1964 and had altogether won seven caps, four of them earlier in 1967. McHarg was in his first season of senior Rugby, but he had already shown much promise. Even so I felt that McCormick, who had now scored 83 points, including the Canadian section, would have a fair chance of reaching his tour century in this game.

MATCH ELEVEN
v. SCOTTISH DISTRICTS
at MELROSE
WEDNESDAY, NOVEMBER 29 1967

Scottish Districts

C. F. Blaikie (Heriot's F. P.)

A. D. Gill (Gala), R. B. Welsh (Hawick), I. Davidson (Langholm), G. J. Keith (Wasps)

B. M. Simmers (Glasgow Academicals), R. C. Allan (Hutchesons' G.S.F.P.)

R. J. Arneil (Edinburgh Academicals), C. W. Thorburn (Guy's Hospital), W. J. Hunter (Hawick), A. F. McHarg (West of Scotland), T. G. Elliot (Langholm), T. K. McDonald (London Scottish), D. T. Deans (Hawick), P. C. Robertson (Hawick)

All Blacks

W. F. McCormick

M. J. Dick, G. S. Thorne, W. M. Birtwistle

G. F. Kember, W. D. Cottrell

C. R. Laidlaw

M. C. Wills, W. J. Nathan, A. E. Smith, B. J. Lochore, capt, K. R. Tremain, E. J. Hazlett, J. Major, A. E. Hopkinson

REFEREE: M. JOSEPH (Wales)

SCOTTISH DISTRICTS 14 POINTS
Try—Gill; conversion—Blaikie; 3 penalty goals—Blaikie

ALL BLACKS 35 POINTS
7 tries—Birtwistle (3), Thorne, Laidlaw, Hopkinson, Nathan; 4 conversions—McCormick; 2 penalty goals—McCormick

One-Way Traffic

AN UNUSUAL prelude to this game was the laying down of disinfected sawdust, near the entrance to the picturesque Greenyards ground, for spectators to walk through. This was yet another precaution against the spread of foot and mouth disease which had by now caused the postponement of a number of representative matches in England in rural areas. By the time of the kick-off a crowd of about 7,000 had been packed into the little ground.

McCormick had early chances to add to his tour total of 83 points. But he failed with three penalty kicks at goal—altogether he was to fail with four in the first half—before Thorne opened the scoring with a fine try. For this the All Blacks first wheeled a scrum and swamped the Scottish scrum-half. Next, Laidlaw whipped the ball out to Cottrell; and then Cottrell and Kember worked a scissors, thus paving the way for Thorne to cut inside on the Scottish 25 and to run on from the right to the posts for a try which McCormick converted (5-0). This was followed by Blaikie's first penalty goal (5-3), but before long Laidlaw initiated and completed a blind-side movement with Birtwistle, and McCormick again converted (10-3). Blaikie's second penalty goal made the score 10-6 at halftime.

At this stage the Districts were holding on bravely. Major had won the tight-head heels by no more than 2-1, Hunter had been doing reasonably well at the line-out, and the All Blacks had not been allowed to have it all their own way at the rucks. Here Robertson, a late replacement for Suddon, set a fine example with his fearless driving. The two penalty goals by Blaikie—who was now wearing a bandage on his head because of a bang received early in the game which required two stitches—were from long range, one of them indeed from more than 50 yards. And of course the Scots had been defending with great courage. Blaikie had done well here too, and Arneil and Elliot, in particular, had done a lot of valuable covering and tackling.

The All Blacks had not been all that convincing. Apart from McCormick's missed kicks, the backs had not been as direct as they could—and should—have been and their handling was not sure. It was from a ball sent loose by a tackle on Thorne in midfield that the Districts, four minutes after the interval, scored the try which really brought the game to life and gave the crowd their one big cheer of the day. After the ball had gone loose, and before the All Blacks could recover, Simmers got a boot to the ball and hacked it upfield. McCormick and Dick both tried unsuccessfully to cope with the situation. Gill, a late replacement for Whyte, raced after the ball and scored a try which Blaikie converted, thus putting the Districts into an unexpected lead of 11-10.

As usual on this tour, however, the All Blacks did not let this breakdown weaken their resolve to keep the ball on the move, and almost immediately they were rewarded with a try. Keith failed to deal with a kick-ahead, the ball bounced off towards the Scottish posts. Three All Blacks went for it, and Hopkinson scored the try converted by McCormick (15-11). After this the All Blacks steadily took over, and their mastery of the rucks took its toll. Birtwistle scored three tries, and Nathan, wrenching his way through attempted tackles, another. McCormick kicked two penalty goals and made a conversion.

It was almost all one-way traffic. Once Keith did come into the Districts' line from the blind side, but the handling broke down in the centre with Gill looking expectantly for the overlap. The only reply for the Scots was Blaikie's third penalty goal. Even Deans, who had hooked with skill, lost the ball three times late in the game on his own side's put-in. Allan had a lot of difficulty in putting the ball in properly. On the credit side for the Scots, McHarg's promise was there for all to see, well-known players like Blaikie and Arneil had done their reputations no harm, and Simmers had had a good game in the circumstances, especially with his accurate kicking. There was some satisfaction, too, in having held the All Blacks to a lead of no more than seven points for an hour. But the

All Blacks had scored 20 points in the last 24 minutes, three tries in the last ten. There was clearly a marked discrepancy in stamina and fitness.

From the All Blacks' point of view, both Tremain and Nathan had played well and were obviously both candidates for the Test against Scotland the following Saturday. Laidlaw too, with his smooth distribution as well as doing almost Going-like probing, had staked a firm claim to reinstatement. On the other hand Dick had strained an Achilles tendon which was to rule him out of the Test team.

Lochore had played a fine game at lock in spite of being injured twice, and he had seemed to bring out the best in Smith. Cottrell had settled down in the second half and played a thoughtfully varied game at first five-eighth, and Kember had then shown some strong straight running. Thorne had made two especially fine breaks, and Birtwistle had scored three tries, all of them admittedly made for him. The All Blacks had now scored 45 tries in 11 games, an average of four per match.

Playing Against History

THE NEW ZEALAND Test team to play Scotland at Murrayfield on Saturday, December 2, showed four changes from the side which had beaten France 21-15 at Colombes the week before. Laidlaw returned in place of Going at halfback; Hopkinson was chosen for his first Test at tight head prop to the exclusion of Muller; Birtwistle came in for Dick on the right wing, and Tremain returned to the place on the flank which Kirkpatrick had filled in Paris.

The most straightforward of the four changes was the substitution of Birtwistle for Dick. There was really no alternative here. Dick was limping badly because of his strained Achilles tendon, and Clarke was still not fit after his thigh trouble. Thus Steel and Birtwistle were the only two fit wings in the party. On the other hand there was now a certain amount of congestion for the flank forward positions. Kirkpatrick was ruled out by the broken nose he had suffered in Paris, but Nathan was now fit again. He and Tremain had both played impressive games at Melrose, but Williams had been playing well all the time Nathan had been nursing his broken jaw. Thus there were three candidates for the two flank positions. It would have been possible to play all three of them by moving Lochore up to partner Meads at lock and choosing Tremain at No. 8. But this would have meant a less effective tail of the line-out just where Scotland were known to be well equipped in the person of Fisher, their captain. The two who were eventually chosen for the flank positions— and it cannot have been an easy decision—were Tremain and Williams, leaving Nathan without a Test appearance of the tour.

There seemed no obvious reason for the choice of Hopkinson in preference to Muller. Both seemed to me to be sound props, neither of them quite as effective a forward as Hazlett at his best. The return of Laidlaw was not unexpected. Going had done himself full justice against France and had had a lot to do with New Zealand's victory. But Laidlaw's skilled passing and his close understanding with Kirton were needed for the fluent open Rugby the All Blacks wanted to play. Laidlaw had reacted to being dropped by giving a highly convincing display against the Scottish Districts at Melrose, and there was a likelihood that his game would be all the sharper now as a result of his non-selection for the French Test.

Elsewhere in the side there was not a great deal of challenge for positions. For all Thorne's promise, Davis was clearly the best man for the centre. Cottrell would not have let the side down at second five-eighth, but in Paris MacRae had played his most impressive game of the tour. Had he not done so, I would at this stage have preferred Cottrell. At lock Strahan was still not as hard as Jennings, but Jennings was not by any means as effective at No. 5 in the line-out as Strahan. This was an especially important consideration for this Test since Scotland had chosen Peter Stagg whose height was now officially given as 6 ft. 10 in. There had never been much to choose between McLeod and Major, but in a fast game, such as these All Blacks aimed to impose, McLeod's relative quickness about the paddock was a strong point in his favour.

In trying to get a side together for Tests, the Scotland selectors are helped by the inter-district matches involving Edinburgh, Glasgow, the South, and the North Midlands. This year they also had a match between Glasgow and a team of Anglo-Scots—that is, a side composed of Scots living and playing for clubs in England—as well as a full-scale trial. This trial took place on the Saturday before the Test, that is to say on the afternoon of November 25, when New Zealand were playing France. The previous season Scotland had made a fine start by beating Australia 11–5 at Murrayfield, France 9–8 at Colombes, and Wales 11–5 at Murrayfield. But after that, without David Chisholm—their stand-off half, who had had to have a knee cartilage operation—they fell away, losing 3–5 to Ireland at Murrayfield and 14–27 to England at Twickenham.

Chisholm had again been injured (in a club match between

Melrose and Hawick) early in the 1967–68 season. This trial, the week before the Scotland-New Zealand Test, was his first match for four weeks. The trial was a fitness test for him, and also a thorough examination for his long established club, district, and Test partnership with Alex Hastie. They had played together in ten Tests and had never been on the losing side together. Hastie was now 32, he had first played for Scotland in 1961, and he had since then taken part in 14 Tests. He himself had twice been on the losing side in Tests, but with a different stand-off half. He had been dropped in the closing stages of the previous season after Chisholm's knee injury, his value to Scotland being primarily in his partnership with Chisholm. The stand-off, too, had now passed 30, and it had yet to be proved that his knee could stand up to the rigours and pace of a Test. It was important for Scotland that he should come through this trial satisfactorily. He had been on winning sides against England, Ireland, Wales, France, South Africa, and Australia.

Another old stager whose form had to be closely watched in this trial was David Rollo at tight head prop. He was now 33 and had first played for Scotland in 1959. Since then he had missed only two Tests, because of injury, and he had already played for Scotland 36 times. If he could gain selection again, he would be hot on the trail of H. F. McLeod's Scottish record of 40 appearances for his country.

This trial was also something of a fitness test for Frank Laidlaw who had recently been injured. Since he had already hooked fourteen times for Scotland and had also played for the 1966 Lions in both the second and third Tests against New Zealand, his experience would be of much value to Scotland. In the event all these players proved themselves fit and in sufficiently good form to be chosen against New Zealand. By winning the trial 26–8 and scoring seven tries in the process, the Blues, who were the senior side and who included 12 men who had played for Scotland the previous season, made the task of the Scottish selectors relatively simple. They picked 14 of the 15 Blues for the Test, the one exception being Keith, the left wing.

The man the selectors brought in in place of Keith was Bob

Keddie, a newcomer aged 22. He had considerable pace to commend him, and he had played for the Scottish Districts side which beat the 1965 Springboks. On that occasion he had had the instructive experience of playing opposite South Africa's Engelbrecht. He had also played for the combined Glasgow and Edinburgh fifteen against the 1966–67 Wallabies. There were two other newcomers in the side: Frame in the centre and Mitchell at lock. Frame, who had made two tries in the trial, was only 21, yet he weighed 14 st. 7 lb. He was also more than 6 ft. tall.

The most unusual player in the side—because of his great height—was Peter Stagg, at lock. He had now completed three seasons (13 games) for Scotland after gaining Blues at Oxford University in 1961 and 1962. Since first being picked for Scotland in 1965 he had missed only one game—against Ireland in his first Test season. During all this time his height appeared in match programmes as 6 ft. 7 in. Having seen how much taller he looked at line-outs than Dauga of France, who was officially credited with 6 ft. 5 in., I always felt Stagg was more than 6 ft. 7 in.

Once, after a trial at Murrayfield, I travelled back in the train with Stagg from Edinburgh to Manchester. Guessing he was sensitive about his height I did not ask him about it, but I could not help noticing, as we walked most of the length of the train to the dining car, that at some parts of the corridor he had to duck. On the walk back to our compartment after the meal I made a careful note of where he could stand upright, where he had to duck, and how far his head was from the ceiling when he was walking normally. When, two or three weeks later, I went up to Murrayfield again for a Test, I remembered to take my wife's tape measure with me. I spent part of the train journey going up the corridor, putting the tape measure against the walls and suspending it from various parts of the ceiling. It must have looked very odd to the people who peered out over their newspapers into the corridor, but my researches convinced me that Stagg was at least 6 ft. 10 in. Now that he has publicly admitted to being 6 ft. 10 in., I don't think he will mind my telling the story. He is almost certainly the tallest Test player of all time, and he has now developed a great deal as an all-round forward. His weight is now given in programmes as 18 stone.

Pringle Fisher, Scotland's captain, had played 20 times for his country since first being picked in 1963. I thought he was unlucky not to be chosen for the 1966 Lions. He was a constructive, ball-playing type of wing forward who had also played basketball for both Scotland and Great Britain. Boyle, at No. 8 was a relative new boy, having played only twice for Scotland, against Australia and France the previous season when Jim Telfer, a 1966 Lion, was injured, as he was now. And Carmichael, at loose head prop, was also inexperienced, having played only once for Scotland. This was against Ireland, early in 1967, when he was given only about an hour's notice before the Scotland-Ireland match that Rollo was unfit. Generally, however, the pack had plenty of experience, for the other wing forward was Derrick Grant who had been on the 1966 Lions' tour to New Zealand and Australia. He had played only eight games in New Zealand, it is true, because of a persistent groin injury, but back home he had played in all Scotland's five matches the following season. The Scottish pack, I thought, might lack power for the set scrums, but it would be well equipped for the line-out and had enough experienced men for the rucks not to be too one-sided.

Hastie and Chisholm could be relied upon to play realistically at halfback, and Turner, who was to be young Frame's partner in the centre, had a stand-off half's fine sense of timing. Turner was normally a stand-off half for his club and played in his first Test as a stand-off half in place of Chisholm who was injured. But for the South of Scotland and for Scotland he had played mainly in the centre. He had played in six Tests. Outside him on the right wing he had Sandy Hinshelwood, who had played in two Tests for the Lions against New Zealand in 1966. Hinshelwood would be playing for Scotland for the tenth time, having first played early in 1966. This threequarter line, with two newcomers in it, was something of an unknown quantity.

At full-back, Stewart Wilson—still only 25—had played 17 times for Scotland as well as in all four Tests against New

Zealand for the 1966 Lions. He was a former captain of Scotland, having taken over the captaincy from Mike Campbell-Lamerton in the middle of the 1964–65 home international championship season, and having himself passed it on to Iain Laughland in the middle of the following season. He was still considered the best full-back in the British Isles. At the time of this Scotland-New Zealand Test his brother was following in his footsteps in gaining a Blue at Oxford University, also at full-back.

So much for the make-up of the teams. History suggested that New Zealanders found great difficulty in crossing Scotland's line. Scotland, in fact, had not conceded a try to New Zealand since November, 1935. When the two countries met in 1954, New Zealand won by a penalty goal (by Bob Scott) to nothing, and the 1964 match produced no score at all. Saxton's Kiwis side of 1945–46 did score a try against Scotland but they lost the match 6–11, one of the only two games they lost out of their total of 33.

It seemed to me that the one thing that was certain about this 1967 match was that Scotland would not this time be able to hold the All Blacks by playing as they did in 1964. On that occasion Scotland played a sober game and concentrated on instantaneous first-time tackling of any New Zealand forward who tried to break from a set scrum, line-out, or ruck. In this way they contained the 1963–64 All Blacks and forced them in the last quarter of an hour or so to try to attack through their backs. But those All Blacks were not used to attacking through their backs direct from set pieces, and consequently they made a hash of their attempts. The 1967 New Zealanders, however, would present a much more complex problem for the Scottish defenders because of their broader vision and their larger field of action.

As I saw it, Scotland's chief hope must be that they might gain a measure of control of the play from their line-out jumpers, provided Scotland were more flexible in their positioning than the French had been the week before, and provided the wings threw in the ball more intelligently and more accurately than the French. How Scotland should use what possession they won was a difficult question. These All Blacks seemed armed to combat whatever type of game their opponents played. One obvious way for Scotland, if they did do well at the line-out, was for Hastie and Chisholm to use the boot to produce more and more line-outs until they were within the range of Chisholm's dropkicking and Wilson's penalty kicking. But this tight type of Rugby was not likely to be enough against a side going all-out to score tries, as the All Blacks were. It seemed that Chisholm would have to exercise his inside break and also to see what this young and largely untried threequarter line of his could do. There were, incidentally, three Scots left from the side which had drawn 0–0 with Whineray's All Blacks. They were Wilson at full back, Rollo at tight head prop, and Fisher at wing forward. The All Blacks were fielding four survivors from that 1964 match, all in the pack—Meads, Gray, Lochore, and Tremain. This was to be Meads's 42nd Test.

Familiar faces seemed to be arriving every minute in Edinburgh. Somehow you seem to be able to see people coming and going more readily in Edinburgh than in London or Cardiff. Neither of those cities has anything to compare with the open vistas of Princes Street, and it is in Princes Street, or on the steps of its hotels, that you meet people. One of Edinburgh's distinguished visitors for the Test was Mike Campbell-Lamerton, captain of the 1966 Lions. There was much amusement when the story got round that the take-off of his flight from London Airport to Edinburgh had been delayed for 25 minutes because of overloading.

It was a dry afternoon, the weather was mild as it had been all week in Edinburgh, and the sun was not far off. The busker, with his drums and his whistles, was performing at his customary pitch in Roseburn Street, and inside the ground the bagpipes and drums of the Queen Victoria School, Dunblane, marching up and down the perfect turf, were as hauntingly impressive as ever. It was a wonderful setting for the last Test of the tour. We did not know then that this was the match that was to bring unwanted controversy to a team which had sailed serene and unblemished through six weeks of touring.

MATCH TWELVE

v. SCOTLAND
at MURRAYFIELD
SATURDAY, DECEMBER 2 1967

Scotland

S.Wilson (London Scottish)

A. J. W. Hinshelwood (London Scottish), J. W. C. Turner (Gala), J. N. M. Frame (Edinburgh University), R. R. Keddie (Watsonians)

D. H. Chisholm (Melrose), A. J. Hastie (Melrose)

A. H. W. Boyle (London Scottish), D. Grant (Hawick), G. W. E. Mitchell (Edinburgh Wanderers), P. K. Stagg (Sale), J. P. Fisher (London Scottish), capt, A. B. Carmichael (West of Scotland), F. A. L. Laidlaw (Melrose), D. M. D. Rollo (Howe of Fife)

New Zealand

W. F. McCormick

W. M. Birtwistle, W. L. Davis, A. G. Steel

I. R. MacRae, E. W. Kirton

C. R. Laidlaw

B. J. Lochore, capt, G. C. Williams, S. C. Strahan, C. E. Meads, K. R. Tremain, K. F. Gray, B. E. McLeod, A. E. Hopkinson

REFEREE: K. D. KELLEHER (Ireland)

SCOTLAND 3 POINTS

Dropped goal—Chisholm

NEW ZEALAND 14 POINTS

2 tries—MacRae, Davis; conversion—McCormick; 2 penalty goals—McCormick

The Great Controversy

UNFORTUNATELY this match will be remembered chiefly as the one in which Colin Meads was sent off three minutes from the end. It was the first time anyone had been sent off in a Test in the British Isles since January 18, 1925, when Cyril Brownlie, also of New Zealand, was dismissed ten minutes after the start of the England-New Zealand Test at Twickenham for allegedly kicking a man who was lying on the ground.

The sending-off of Colin Meads, and the management's treatment of the affair, created a controversy which sent indignant outbursts and strongly worded cables booming from one side of the world to the other. All the hullabaloo inevitably obscured the quality of a match which was in its own right an interesting and exciting contest, a Test different from the other three but not less absorbing. Let us therefore deal first with the match, to which the Meads affair, coming as it did after all the scoring had been completed and only three minutes from the end, was more or less an appendage.

What made the game especially interesting, and significant perhaps for the future of Rugby, was Scotland's repeated use of a mini line-out consisting of four men: Laidlaw, Mitchell, Stagg, and Fisher. When Stagg, with his 6 ft. 10 in., jumps high and goes for the ball one-handed, it can safely be said that no Test player can outreach him. When there are so few people to clutter the line-out, it is difficult for opponents to apply illegal impediments with impunity. The referee has a much clearer view of the proceedings. Even so the Scottish wings, knowing that Stagg could be legally prevented from getting the ball cleanly to his scrum-half, varied their throw-in to keep the All Blacks guessing.

In marked contrast to the French and their unintelligent throwing-in the week before at Colombes, the Scottish wings now sometimes threw the ball beyond Stagg to Fisher—and occasionally sent it right over both of them for Hastie to chase. The All Blacks countered by bringing in five men to mark Scotland's four—McLeod, Gray, Meads, Strahan, and Lochore—but Scotland, having the throw-in, could dictate the length of the line-out and so cramp the New Zealanders. It was a fascinating little battle, and New Zealand seldom got the ball back from Scotland's mini line-outs.

When Scotland had the throw-in at an orthodox eight-man line-out, they were not anything like so successful. Their least successful ploy was a clearly-planned manoeuvre in which the wing threequarter appeared to be about to throw to Stagg at No. 5 in the line—but instead sent the ball shorter to Mitchell at No. 3 while Stagg got ready to put his head down and to help in the binding and supporting. This move often came to grief because Mitchell was outsmarted by the All Blacks.

When New Zealand had the throw-in, however, the Scots again could make life awkward for the All Blacks. Stagg's reach enabled him sometimes to beat Strahan for the ball at No. 5 and to pull it down to Mitchell at No. 3. Occasionally Fisher would get the better of Lochore at the tail of the line. And in sharp contrast to the rigid positioning of the French line-out forwards, Stagg was prepared to watch Lochore and then to move quickly forward if the ball was going instead to Strahan at No. 5. New Zealand got enough of the ball to win the match, of course, but it was heartening to see a country where coaching is popularly supposed to be frowned upon offer the best organised line-out play of the four countries New Zealand met.

It says much for the will-power of Saxton, passed on through the medium of Lochore, that in spite of Scotland's crushingly tight defence and their alertness for the counter-thrust, the All Blacks still went on playing attacking Rugby and scored a very fine try five minutes from the end. Ultimately this singlemindedness, their grand teamwork, and their superior basic technique took them to a hard-won victory. Some people thought the All Blacks did not play well and that this was their least good Test win. It seemed to me to be the perfect example of a side playing only as well as it was allowed to. Scotland put up a magnificent resistance, and to beat them 14-3 was a genuine triumph for the All Blacks.

The first thrusts of the game were made by New Zealand. They won the first line-out from a Scottish throw-in, and Kirton kicked diagonally to the right. There they won another line-out, and Meads charged away with the ball round the back leftwards. When he was checked, Laidlaw switched the ball back towards the right where Kirton grubkicked. There was now a brief delay while Meads changed torn shorts, and then Kirton came into the line a second time. Here the first show of Scottish defiance: Kirton was not only held, but Frame grabbed the ball and found a long touch. Next, Scotland worked on another loose ball. Wilson came up as an overlap; but he dropped the ball. Then the Scots tried a mini four-man line-out and Tremain, who had retired the necessary 10 yards, started running forwards again too soon. Wilson's long penalty kick fell just short.

New Zealand by this time were having to throw the ball in short at some line-outs to Gray at No. 2 to keep it away from Stagg. On one such occasion Stagg came forward himself to No. 2, with the result that Steel's throw-in either was not straight or did not go five yards. So there was a set scrum on Scotland's right with Scotland to put in. Scotland heeled, Hastie unerringly found Chisholm, and Chisholm, after a little feint, dropped a fine goal with his left foot (3-0).

Chisholm was soon attacking again, this time with a run and grubkick on the blind side of a set scrum, but then New Zealand used the blind side—Laidlaw passing direct to Mac-Rae with Kirton following him round close to the touchline. Nothing came of this, but shortly afterwards the Scottish backs were caught standing offside while a line-out was taking place, and McCormick was presented with a simple penalty goal (3-3).

Another run by Chisholm created a promising situation, but Boyle knocked on. Davis lost the ball in trying to kick it through, Keddie ran off with it and crosskicked, and the pressure was on New Zealand. They threw the ball in short to a line-out and smuggled it to Tremain who forced his way up the touchline, but Chisholm ran on the blind side and kicked back to the open side. The pressure was on again. This time they cleared more completely, and soon Kirton was running wide and passing inside to MacRae. Soon, too, Meads took a tap-down from a line-out on the right, Gray was at his elbow and in his turn charged ahead. When pace was needed to complete the move, up came MacRae for a flawlessly-constructed try on the left after half an hour's play (6-3).

At this stage of the game there was a flash of genius from Chris Laidlaw which reminded me of Haydn Tanner, the great Welsh scrum-half who was only 18 when he helped Wales to beat New Zealand 13-12 at Cardiff in 1935 and who was still playing for Wales in 1949. Laidlaw made a quick dart to the blind side: while he was on his way he let fly a superb reverse pass right out to Kirton on the open side. It was shortly after this that the All Backs swamped Hastie, a Scot offended at the ruck, and McCormick kicked his second penalty goal (9-3). Each side had the chance of a score between then and halftime. Meads barged the would-be catcher of the ball from a drop-out before the ball arrived, and Wilson missed with the difficult penalty kick. Tremain picked up the ball from a Scottish heel at a set scrum and dived over the Scotland line, but he had knocked on in picking up.

The second half began typically with Lochore tapping the ball down from the back of a line-out, Laidlaw getting his backs away with a swift pass, Davis being fiercely tackled in the centre, and the Scots taking the ball upfield at their feet. Then there were a series of mistakes. MacRae knocked on in a line movement, Kirton knocked on and when Boyle picked up the ball at the back of a Scottish scrum and ran with it, Hastie dropped his pass. The defences were unyielding at this stage, and under pressure the handling of both sides became unsure.

At last the Scots launched a promising move. In fact it was the move the Lions had used in making that splendid try for Hinshelwood in the last Test at Auckland in 1966. Frame, the inside centre, was missed out in a movement begun from a line-out on the left, and Wilson came into the line outside Turner. Unfortunately for Scotland, Wilson could not quite hold on to a difficult pass.

At this point, Scotland had to make do briefly without

Frame who hurt a leg. Hinshelwood was brought into the centre, and Grant moved to the right wing. But Frame was back before Tremain picked up the ball at a set scrum and sent Laidlaw and Steel off on a nice manoeuvre on the blind side. Next Lochore carried his ploy of standing out of a set scrum a stage further. Opponents had been hearing about this move by now so, while Lochore stood ostentatiously out on the open side, Laidlaw sent the ball instead direct to McCormick who was running on the blind side. Somehow the Scots frustrated even this, and then they won two line-outs in quick succession from New Zealand throw-ins. After the first Chisholm found a long touch, and after the second Scotland tried that Lions move again. Once more, however, their handling was not quite good enough.

It was fitting that the All Blacks' sense of timing, sense of direction, and handling skill should all be seen at their best in their last move of the day. From a line-out on the right on Scotland's 25 the ball went from Laidlaw to Kirton to MacRae who swung slightly inwards; Kirton came into the line a second time outside MacRae, ran straight through the gap, and put Davis over for a very fine try (12-3). In spite of a shocking din from the crowd, McCormick converted from well out on the left.

That try would have made a beautiful ending to the last Test of the tour. Sadly, the ugliness of controversy now had to intrude. It was from a loose scrum following the kick-off after this try that the Meads incident occurred. It happened in the open where all could see. The loose scrum was on Scotland's left of the field, and the ball came back from it towards Chisholm who stooped to pick it up. As the ball was on its way back, Meads broke free from the scrum and ran to challenge Chisholm for possession. On arriving in the vicinity of Chisholm and the ball, Meads let fly a powerful kick, and both he and Chisholm fell to the ground.

My own immediate reaction at this moment, before I knew that the referee had even seen the incident, was that Meads was feigning injury in the hope of leniency from the referee. Mr Kelleher came up and spoke firmly to Meads, who trudged promptly off the field. I was very surprised that he had been sent off, because punishment for this type of dangerous play is usually limited to a caution. I did not know then that Mr Kelleher had given Meads a formal warning earlier in the game.

As this was the first time anyone had been sent off in a Test since 1925, there was bound to be a commotion. When Charlie Saxton, having seen the television film of the incident three times, said later the same evening that the sending-off of Meads was quite unjustified, the fat was really in the fire. Everyone, I think, was united in a feeling of sorrow at seeing such a great player as Meads sent off, but there were many shades of opinion about the offence. Here are some of them.

Saxton himself said: *'The incident was grossly exaggerated. Meads was trying to play the ball with his foot just as Chisholm was picking it up. Chisholm himself was the first to say this when he came to our dressing room to see Meads. The decision was most uncalled for. It was not the sort of game which needed a supreme example to be made of anyone. After seeing the television film of the incident three times, I am more convinced than ever that a great injustice has been done to a great player'.*

The referee said: *'About threequarters of the way through the first half I gave Meads a formal warning. I had just seen him walk on the backs of two or three players as they lay on the ground at a loose scrummage. I told him this was a last warning. When I saw the incident involving Chisholm, I had no other option under the laws of Rugby but to order him off the field.'*

Norman Mair, in *The Scotsman*, quoted a 'famous referee' as saying that after the incident as he saw it Mr Kelleher was bound to send Meads off.

I wrote in *The Guardian*: *'I have never thought Meads a dirty player. He is a very hard player and an intensely keen one. He sometimes goes a bit too far in his keenness, as I believe he did on Saturday. To kick as powerfully as he did when Chisholm was so close seemed to me to constitute dangerous play, irrespective of Meads's intention. But the referee, who apparently had spoken twice to Meads, is the sole judge of that. It would be quite wrong to suggest that Saturday's international was a dirty game, just as it would be quite wrong to label these All Blacks a dirty team. Saturday's match was a picnic compared with the game in Paris the week before. The great irony is that on Saturday Meads was wearing a scrum cap expressly to protect a wound inflicted in Paris when a French boot crashed against his head far away from the ball. That incident was not noticed by the referee.'*

In *The Daily Telegraph* John Reason wrote: '*The kick missed both the ball and Chisholm, but the referee, who was about five yards away, felt that Meads was indifferent whether he hit either. Meads had already been formerly cautioned for trampling on players in a ruck in the first half, so by law Mr Kelleher had no alternative but to send him off the field. Meads certainly plays the game hard and he has been lucky in the past. On this occasion, though, I think he was unlucky. In my opinion there was an element of dangerous play about Meads's action, but I doubt whether it was wilful.'*

Cliff Morgan wrote in *The News of the World*: '*Having warned Meads in the first half, Irish referee Kevin Kelleher, under the laws of Rugby, was required to give him his marching orders. I had the feeling that the decision was slightly swayed by the fact that a reputation for robust play had preceded Meads to this country.'*

In *The Daily Express*, Pat Marshall wrote: '*Colin Meads got a raw deal . . . I think he should not have been sent off . . . "A miscarriage of justice", was Saxton's verdict. I agree.'*

In *The Daily Mail*, J. L. Manning said: '*Of course it was a deliberate foul by Meads. If it is argued that Mr Kelleher observed the letter of the law, but not its spirit, may I ask why this is the letter if it is not also intended to be the spirit? And who can believe after watching the way Meads played in this match that this is intended to be the spirit of Rugby?*

The Times, which devoted half a page to the affair, carried comments by U. A. Titley, their Rugby correspondent, Terry McLean, of *The New Zealand Herald*, John Downie, a former Rugby correspondent of *The Glasgow Herald*, and Paul MacWeeney, sports editor of *The Irish Times*. Titley wrote: '*Many people thought that the referee's decision was harsh, and there was certainly one Scottish forward who was no* saint. *Moreover, Meads may have reflected ironically, on the Frenchman who had with impunity kicked his head open a week before. But it is well to try to keep a rare occurrence like Saturday's in perspective ... Meads had already been formally warned for dangerous play by a referee who made it clear, quite early, that he was going to stand no nonsense. Prudence, therefore, should have been his watchword thenceforth. The experienced referee himself showed considerable courage in acting as he did in such high-powered circumstances.'*

Terry McLean: *'The various New Zealand points of view could be reduced in essence to the belief that Mr Kelleher was at fault in exacting so severe a penalty. In the light of Mr Kelleher's distinguished career as a referee, no New Zealander could doubt his qualifications for the match, for which, incidentally, he was chosen by the All Blacks themselves. But there is a passionate belief that Mr Kelleher, either because he was unsighted or because he was affected by the sudden outbreak of ill temper in both packs, too rapidly and hastily reached the judgement that Meads had committed an act of dangerous play. It is deeply believed by the All Blacks that Meads was legitimately attempting to kick the ball out of Chisholm's grasp.'*

John Downie: *'Meads had been warned in the first half for trampling on an opponent, he had escaped punishment in the second half for a kick, again aimed at the ball, that almost struck Hastie in the face, and in the final incident he was guilty of more than one offence. Having entered the ruck from the wrong side, he was hauled out by Carmichael. Presumably Mr Kelleher did not penalise him for offside because Scotland had gained the advantage of the heel, but the advantage was nullified by the kick that made the referee call enough. No one can dispute that all experienced reporters of Rugby have seen more culpable incidents in international matches go unpunished. But no number of wrongs make a right . . . Perhaps if this unquestionably great player had been ordered off earlier in his international career his subsequent play would not have contained the element of recklessness that has repeatedly alarmed and annoyed British spectators.'*

Paul MacWeeney: *'Mr Kelleher is the headmaster of a*

Dublin boys' preparatory school and is honorary secretary of the Leinster Schools section. In invoking the severest penalty on Meads he was applying law 20, section 2 (c) of the Laws of Rugby football, which states, in effect, that if a player, after warning, commits a further offence against the spirit of the game he must *be sent off.'*

It seemed to me on the weekend of the Meads incident that there was a climate of opinion forming against Mr Kevin Kelleher. This I think was largely because of Saxton's appearance on television protesting Meads's innocence and the prominence given in the Sunday papers to his statement that the sending-off was unjustified.

I thought it necessary to point out that, after Mr Gwynne Walters of Wales, Kelleher was the most experienced active top-class referee in the British Isles. This Scotland-New Zealand game was the sixteenth Test he had refereed since he took the Wales v Scotland match in the 1959–60 season. He had taken at least one Test every season since then, and in addition had twice refereed games between France and Rumania. In January, 1964, he had refereed the previous All Blacks against Ulster in Belfast where they won 24-5. In the 1966–67 season he had taken four of the first six Tests including England's and Wales's Tests against Australia.

Over the weekend it was announced that the Meads case would be considered by an Adjudication Committee appointed by the International Rugby Football Board. The committee would meet the following Tuesday in Cardiff, where the All Blacks would be staying for the week, and the three-man committee would include Saxton. A hectic affair seemed temporarily to have come to a halt.

Verdict on Meads

THE HALT was of the briefest kind, for the announcement of the All Blacks' team to play Monmouthshire at Newport the following Wednesday heaped controversy upon controversy. Meads was included in the side. It was easy to understand that those in the party who believed Meads had not committed any offence should want to express their belief in his innocence by naming him for the next match. But to do so was to take a narrow view. Whatever one's opinion about the rights and wrongs of the sending-off incident, the sending-off itself was a fact. For an international side deliberately to choose for their very next match a player who had just been sent off, and whose case was about to be heard, did seem to be setting a poor example to the officers at representative and club level who strive to keep the game healthy.

Saxton said simply: 'This is the team that we have selected and the one that we want to play on next Wednesday.' Saxton, admirably tough little man that he is, would no doubt take all the responsibility for the decision to include Meads in the side to play at Newport. But the decision was out of character for a man with such a wide understanding and firm grasp of the affairs of Rugby. I feel that on this occasion he must have allowed himself to accept bad advice.

The team chosen for this match against Monmouthshire was the most experienced the All Blacks had picked for any midweek match on the tour. McCormick was at full-back, and the threequarters, as originally selected, read Dick, Davis, Steel. The five-eighths were Kirton and Cottrell, and Going was at halfback. With Lochore at No. 8, Tremain and Nathan on the flanks, Meads and Jennings at lock, and Gray, Major, and Muller in the front row, the All Blacks could scarcely have chosen a more experienced pack.

The reasons behind the choosing of such a strong side could be seen partly in the past and partly in the present. Monmouthshire had beaten Saxton's Kiwis 15-0 in February, 1946. It was, incidentally, an odd coincidence that within the space of four days the All Blacks should meet both the only two sides to whom Saxton's Kiwis lost—Scotland and Monmouthshire. The Newport club had inflicted their only defeat on Whineray's All Blacks in October, 1963, by a dropped goal (by Uzzell) to nothing. The Welsh are great respecters of tradition, and this alone offered a big challenge to Lochore's All Blacks.

As far as the present was concerned, Monmouthshire were known to have been preparing for a long time for this match. As long ago as the previous August they had appointed David Harries, of Newbridge, as their coach and had issued the names of a squad of 25 players for him to coach. The chosen Monmouthshire fifteen included only four Test players— Brian Price, Denzil Williams, Dennis Hughes, and Keith Jarrett—but the All Blacks had every reason to respect Jarrett, who had the reputation of being the best placekicker in the British Isles. He missed the Wales-New Zealand Test because of injury, but was now fully fit.

Brian Price, at lock, had captained Newport in that victory over the 1963–64 All Blacks. Although he was no longer in the Welsh Test team, he had now the experience of the 1966 Lions tour to New Zealand behind him. Denzil Williams, who was to play at loose head prop, had also been on the Lions tour and on it had played in both Tests against Australia and three of the four in New Zealand. Hughes had recently played at blind side wing forward for Wales against New Zealand— his first Test. His brother, Arthur Hughes, at open side wing forward, had scored more than 100 tries for Newbridge. Here then was a pack with a fair amount of experience.

The backs had fewer big reputations. Ken Jones, in the centre, was not to be confused with the men of the same name who have been on two Lions tours to New Zealand, in 1950 and 1966. The one playing for Monmouthshire was aged 25 and had been playing for Newbridge for five years. Jarrett, though his only cap for Wales had been won the previous season as a full-back, was a regular centre for the Newport club and was picked for Monmouthshire on the left wing. Playing as a centre for Newport he had so far scored 103 points in 13 matches. It was hoped locally that the coaching of Dai Harries would enable the backs to play above their collective reputations.

It was hoped, too, that coaching would put into the background a none-too-convincing record and the loss of several outstanding players. In their preparation, indeed, Monmouthshire had lost both to Gloucestershire and to Glamorgan. Among the players they had lost were Alun Pask and Haydn Morgan, who had retired, and David Watkins, who had gone to Rugby League—all of them former Lions. So the teams were chosen, and we now awaited the outcome of the Tuesday meeting of the International Board's Adjudication Committee concerned with the sending-off of Meads.

The two members of the Adjudication Committee, in addition to Saxton, were Mr Glyn Morgan (Wales) and Mr C. H. Gadney (England). Morgan was president of the Welsh Rugby Union, and Gadney was a former president of the Rugby Football Union. Gadney was one of England's two representatives on the International Board—the other was Mr D. H. Harrison—and he was also a former international referee. He was also a member of both the Laws Committee and the Executive Committee of the R.F.U.

Many people in Britain thought that Saxton should not sit on this committee after publicly expressing the opinion that Meads had been the victim of an injustice. Some even said that to express such an opinion while the matter was, so to speak, *sub judice* amounted almost to contempt of court. I did not feel strongly about this, but I did think it a pity that Saxton's statement that the sending-off was unjustified, together with the naming of Meads for the game at Newport, meant that the public would view the committee meeting as a battle between Saxton and the rest.

The news from the committee was contained in a statement signed by all three members of the committee and issued by Mr V. E. Kirwan (Ireland), the secretary of the International Board. It read: *'The referee, Mr K. D. Kelleher of Ireland,*

*having formally warned C. E. Meads of New Zealand for
foul play and misconduct earlier in the game, making clear
any repetition would mean dismissal from the playing enclo-
sure, is supported in the action he took. Meads has been
severely admonished and warned as to his future conduct and
is suspended for the next two games of the tour.'*

A suspension for two games seemed to me admirably suited
to the situation. It was not a severe sentence. From Meads's
point of view, it meant that he would have to miss the game
against Monmouthshire at Newport and the match against
East Wales, due to be played at Cardiff the following Saturday. But he would not be deprived of a chance of playing in
the last match of the tour—against the Barbarians at Twickenham—and so would have the opportunity of showing the
British public, probably for the last time, just what a great
player he can be. Those of us who admired Meads were glad
that, to that extent, the committee had been lenient.

From a referee's point of view, a two-match suspension had
just enough sting in it to uphold the respect without which no
man can properly referee a Test. It made it clear that dangerous play would not be tolerated, and it put into practice the
feelings expressed by the International Board at their previous
annual meeting, in London in March, 1967. After that meeting the Board issued a statement which said among other
things: *'The International Board is concerned about the
evidence that the standard of play generally is not as good
as it ought to be. The Board considers that this situation arises
from a failure by players to observe certain fundamental laws
of the game, and by referees to enforce these laws uniformly
and consistently, if necessary by the imposition of the extreme
penalty. The main matters to which the board directs the
attention of all players and referees are as follows: 1, Failure
to bind effectively . . . 2, Failure to observe the offside law . . .
3, Over-vigorous and foul play . . . Unions and all affiliated
bodies and clubs must accept responsibility for imposing
discipline on players who are not prepared to play the game
fairly, in accordance with the laws.'*

It now remained for confidence in Mr Kelleher to be shown
by an invitation to him to referee another Test as soon as

convenient. In the event it was announced, later the same week, that he would be the referee of the very first match of the home international championship, between Scotland and France at Murrayfield on January 13.

The statement giving the decision about the two-match suspension could have been expected to bring the Meads case to a close. But Fred Allen was not yet satisfied: *'In my opinion Colin Meads is completely innocent of the charge that he kicked a man,'* he said. He added that Meads had been given an unjustified reputation over the years for over-vigorous play and in his opinion this could have had a bearing on Mr Kelleher's action at Murrayfield: *'I am certain that referees have been singling him out for special attention because of this undeserved reputation.'*

This was a serious charge against the referees of the British Isles and one difficult to substantiate. Allen went on: *'Meads has played clean and fair Rugby all the way through this tour and, even when he has been a victim of aggression, has not overstepped the mark. I was upset on Saturday night and am even more upset now, especially when this means Meads, a great player, will miss his one hundredth game for New Zealand on the tour.'*

The Test against Scotland was in fact Meads's 98th game in an All Black jersey. Now only the Barbarians match was left for him to play in. *'I think Meads might have been given a caution or perhaps a reprimand for the ordering-off—and only then because the committee would back the referee—but not a suspension of two matches,'* Allen added. These were untimely words. They did not help the public to forget the Meads incident, which should have been the object of the All Blacks' management at this stage.

Some people at the time, notably Mr Tom Pearce, former president of the New Zealand Rugby Union, were quoted as saying that Meads had been denied justice because he was not given the right to defend himself. In fact he was given the option, but it was agreed that Saxton should speak on his behalf.

The immediate result of the suspension was that a replacement had to be chosen for Meads in the match against Monmouthshire at Newport next day, and it was Strahan who was called in to partner Jennings at lock. Dick's Achilles tendon trouble would not allow him to play, and since Clarke and Birtwistle were both unfit, Dick's place on the wing was given to Thorne. He was to play on the right and Steel on the left.

There was some rain before the kick-off, but the traditions of the previous matches played by New Zealanders in Monmouthshire, together with the record of the present All Blacks ensured a big crowd. There was local pride, too, in the fact that Monmouthshire was the only individual county honoured with a fixture against Lochore's side. The programme statisticians pointed out that, in five official tours to Europe before this one, teams from New Zealand had lost only nine of 151 matches and six of those defeats had been suffered in Wales. The most recent of those defeats, that suffered at Newport by Whineray's side in 1963, will have been in most people's minds as Lochore's men took the field. They included six of those who had played in the 1963 match—Lochore, Tremain, Nathan, Major, Kirton, and Davis.

MATCH THIRTEEN

v. MONMOUTHSHIRE
at NEWPORT
WEDNESDAY, DECEMBER 6, 1967

Monmouthshire

B. Edwards (Ebbw Vale)

L. Daniels (Pontypool), K. Jones (Newbridge), A. Lewis (Ebbw Vale), K. S. Jarrett (Newport)

M. Grindle (Ebbw Vale), G. Turner (Ebbw Vale)

D. Hughes (Newbridge), capt., A. Hughes (Newbridge), B. Price (Newport), E. Phillips (Newbridge), P. Watts (Newport), D. Williams (Ebbw Vale), B. Wilkins (Abertillery), G. Howls (Ebbw Vale)

All Blacks

W. F. McCormick

G. S. Thorne, W. L. Davis, A. G. Steel

W. D. Cottrell, E. W. Kirton

S. M. Going

B. J. Lochore, capt., W. J. Nathan, A. G. Jennings, S. C. Strahan, K. R. Tremain, K. F. Gray, J. Major, B. L. Muller

REFEREE: G. C. LAMB (England)

MONMOUTHSHIRE 12 POINTS

4 penalty goals—Jarrett

ALL BLACKS 23 POINTS

4 tries—Kirton, Steel, Tremain, Muller; conversion —McCormick; 3 penalty goals—McCormick

ALL BLACKS V. MONMOUTHSHIRE

Revenge Without Beauty

THE ARRIVAL through the ground's North-East gate of a marching column of drummers and pipers dressed in Scottish plaid suggested they had been on the move since the previous Saturday. The failure of the 80-strong combined bands to follow *God Save The Queen* with *Land of my Fathers* leant further credence to the theory. The crowd, however, were not going to be done out of *Land of my Fathers*: as the bands made their musical exit from the paddock, their notes were swamped by Welsh voices in song. The sun came out, Monmouthshire won the toss, and they decided to give Jarrett the benefit of the wind in the first half.

Jarrett's first kick at goal came only five minutes from the start and was from a long way out. It followed one of those decisions which would have gone the other way in another country. Wilkins, the Monmouthshire hooker, did not get off the ball in a loose scrum and therefore came in for some rough treatment. In New Zealand, quite rightly in my opinion, he would have been penalised for not getting away from the ball. In Britain, referees tend not to penalise players for staying on the ball but to blow against the boot which tries to rake the opponent off the ball. In this instance it was the New Zealanders who were penalised, not Wilkins. Jarrett failed with the difficult kick, but not by much. The referee, incidentally, had previously officiated at the very fine match the All Blacks had played against France B at Toulouse. There he was a Group Captain in the Air Force. Now he appeared on the programme as an Air Commodore.

A diagonal kick to the right by Kirton put the All Blacks well into the Monmouthshire 25, but two fine leaps by Brian Price at consecutive line-outs enabled the Welsh to clear their lines. It was noticeable that Monmouthshire already had their open side wing forward stationed out among their backs as an extra midfield defender when the All Blacks were throwing the ball in. Thus they were following the example of France, but so far Jarrett was not kicking as well as Villepreux. After eighteen minutes' play Major was penalised at a set scrum, but Jarrett missed with what was quite a simple kick at goal.

Three minutes later Jennings played the ball in an offside position as it came out of a ruck on the Welsh side, and this time Jarrett did kick the penalty goal from an easy position. Straight from the kick-off after this, however, Nathan and Lochore raced off with the ball. Monmouthshire got offside at the maul following the check, and McCormick answered Jarrett in kind (3-3). Nathan then tapped the ball down to Tremain from the tail of a line-out. Jennings promoted a ruck from which the ball was switched back towards the touchline where Steel and Nathan ran. Nathan was hurt in doing this, and during the brief delay for repairs there came the somewhat incongruous announcement: 'Will Bob Scott and Jack Finlay please come to the committee box after the game.' Great names at a famous place.

Jarrett's fourth penalty kick at goal was taken from several yards inside his own half after Kirton had advanced beyond the hindmost foot of a set scrum. This kick was both short and wide, but the All Blacks were giving him chances. They asserted some authority by holding the ball in a set scrum and walking Monmouthshire back and back until Watts was caught offside, but they were not within range of goal. Moreover, before they could get within range, Nathan left the tail of a line-out too soon in aiming for a throw-in which went over the top. This time, after 31 minutes' play, Jarrett was successful (6-3 to Monmouthshire).

As before, McCormick was not long in kicking a penalty goal in reply, the Monmouthshire centres having been caught offside when Stahan delayed letting the ball back from a line-out (6-6). But, in the last eight minutes of the first half, Jarrett kicked two more penalty goals without reply (12-6 to Monmouthshire). The first came when Major was penalised in the loose and the second was for foot-up by the All Blacks' front row at a set scrum.

I imagine there were many people who during the interval

believed that history was repeating itself and that the All Blacks were again being beaten in Wales. The locals certainly had a good deal of evidence to support such a belief. The All Blacks' handling in midfield had not been as reliable as usual and McCormick's entries into the line had lacked their former slickness. There was also this tendency to be penalised and so to feed Monmouthshire's most potent weapon—the place-kicking of Jarrett.

Monmouthshire, for their part, were quick to take advantage of the All Blacks' handling errors, alertly booting the ball up the paddock and so taking play back to an area from which Jarrett could kick a goal if the All Blacks offended. It was not a very constructive play, but they could not do much in the way of planned attacking—their forwards were not able to get them much clean possession from the set scrums, from the line-outs, or from the rucks. At the set scrums in particular, the All Blacks' method—wheeling the scrum on their opponents' put-in so that Tremain, on the left flank, could impede the operations of the opposing scrum half without having to get offside—was working well. Thus Monmouth-shire were severely limited in their choice of what to do and when. But they stuck to their spoiling and tackling with re-markable singlemindedness. These tactics had certainly worked in this first half, at the end of which they were leading 12-6: all the 18 points having come from penalty goals.

Those of us who had seen a lot of the All Blacks' games, however, knew how well this side could turn on the pressure in the last quarter. We knew the pounding the Monmouthshire pack was taking, and we expected the All Blacks to gain complete command forward in the second half. We also ex-pected Jarrett to get fewer chances of kicking goals in the second half now that the wind would be against him and his team.

In the event it was a long time after the interval before the All Blacks justified this confidence. Monmouthshire were still in the lead (12-9) when more than 20 minutes of the second half had gone. And the All Blacks did not take the lead for the first time in the match until fifteen minutes from the end. It was noticeable after the interval that the All Blacks were now doing more kicking. A high Garryowen penalty kick by Going had the Monmouthshire full back in difficulties. This was followed a minute later by a high kick to the left by Kirton. Monmouthshire had to do without Watts for a few minutes because of a damaged knee, and it was while he was off the paddock that Kirton scored one of the best individual tries of the whole tour. Kirton, of course, had been made something of a scapegoat for the All Blacks' defeat at Newport in 1963. That game had been his first ever in an All Black jersey. If he felt he still had to do something to live down the memories of the 1963–64 tour, he could hardly have done so more emphatically than with this truly breathtaking try.

In a movement begun from a set scrum on the right, Kirton slipped into the line a second time outside his second five-eighth as cleanly and as surely as he had at Murrayfield the previous Saturday. The break this time was made on the Monmouthshire 10-yard line, going left. After he had gone through, Kirton was faced by the cover of Grindle, but he brushed his attempted tackle aside, swept on and on through or past all the rest of the cover, and dived over near the left-hand corner. It was a try which reminded me of the one David Watkins made and scored for the 1966 Lions at Nelson. It did not start in the same way, but it had the same quality about it of mental stamina and concentration. Very few backs, having made the initial break and also beaten the first line of cover, have, in my experience, had the mental strength to dodge past a further wave of defenders and to score a try. In the context of this hitherto unyielding Monmouthshire defence this was a stupendous effort by Kirton.

This made the score 12-9 to Monmouthshire after eight minutes of the second half, and it was followed by another good move. While Kirton ran to the left, Going passed direct to Cottrell who was running right. McCormick came up and Thorne was given a run, but Jennings knocked on his inside pass. Then Going broke from a ruck and dived for the line; but he did not quite get there.

Two unusual incidents followed. First Monmouthshire tried to lure the All Blacks offside by getting their scrum-half to break wide of a scrum without the ball. The All Blacks were not to be fooled and Tremain gratefully picked up the ball. Then Strahan, lashing out with his fists, found himself to his surprise being held back by the referee himself. The referee, presumably sensing provocation, took no action other than awarding a penalty kick to Monmouthshire. This proved to be the only penalty kick at goal which the All Blacks allowed Jarrett in the second half.

Nathan almost got over after a Garryowen by Kirton, Gray was stopped just short, and then the All Blacks took the score to 12-12 after 23 minutes of the second half with another fine try. This came from Lochore doing his trick of standing out of a set scrum. Welsh Rugby fans, of course, had seen him do this before now and had watched him pass to either one of his five-eighths running on each side of him. Now he did what he did at Murrayfield. That is to say he made his position on the open side obvious to the opposition while Going instead passed the ball directly to blind side, to McCormick who had come up surreptitiously. McCormick ran briefly before putting Steel over for a cleverly contrived try.

By now the All Blacks were applying their customary last-quarter pressure. After Kirton had just missed with a long dropkick at goal, Monmouthshire were penalised at a set scrum and McCormick kicked a long and difficult goal, putting them into the lead for the first time (15-12). Next Cottrell knocked on at the line after a Garryowen by Kirton had been fumbled by the Welsh defence, and then McCormick just failed with another penalty kick at goal. After this unsuccessful kick, Monmouthshire tried to drop-out the 'wrong' way and Tremain grabbed the ball and forced his way over for a try (18-12). Finally Gray plunged ahead after taking a tap-down at the back of a line-out, Lochore caught a high bounce with great skill, and Muller supported him for a try converted by McCormick (23-12).

As a game it was not a thing of much beauty. Kirton probably kicked more in this match than in any other. But his try and the try Lochore and McCormick made for Steel could not have been bettered. Revenge for that 1963 defeat had been firmly gained.

Injuries Call the Tune

BECAUSE OF the cancellation of the two Irish matches, the game against East Wales—due to be played at Cardiff Arms Park on Saturday, December 9—had become the last game but one of the tour. The last was to be against the Barbarians the following Saturday, no match having been organised to replace the midweek Irish fixture. Inevitably eyes were already looking forward to the Barbarians match as the great finale, but the Welsh were looking upon this game at Cardiff as their own chance to say farewell and to give the All Blacks a game to remember.

The All Blacks chose an interesting team, partly dictated by injury. Thus Steel and Thorne were to be the wings for the second successive game with Davis in the centre. Herewini, who had been told not to play again on the tour and had not played since the match at Bayonne, was passed fit to play at Cardiff. In the absence of MacRae, who had been having trouble with a back injury, Kember was given a game at second five-eighth, the position he had previously filled only once on the tour, against the Scottish Districts at Melrose. The chosen pack was that which had played in the French Test, with the exceptions of Smith for Meads at lock and Hopkinson for Muller at prop. This meant the return at flanker of Kirkpatrick, who had broken his nose in Paris. The only previous time those two relative youngsters, Strahan and Smith, had been paired at lock was at Bristol in the third match of the tour. Hopkinson and McLeod were both hurt in training. Hopkinson pulled a hamstring and had to be replaced by Hazlett: McLeod hurt a knee and Major took his place.

The qualification for the East Wales team was stretched to cover Welshmen playing for clubs in England. Thus the side, as originally announced, included Raybould, Young, Gray, I. C. Jones and R. Jones. Raybould, a London Welsh centre, had recently played for Wales against New Zealand. Young, the captain of Harrogate and of Yorkshire, had been given a false alarm to get ready to fly out to join the 1966 Lions when Kennedy, one of the Lions' hookers, was wrongly thought to have broken his jaw at Wellington. I. C. Jones, a South African lock had won a Blue at Oxford in 1962, 1963, and 1964 and was currently playing for London Welsh. R. Jones, of Coventry and Warwickshire, had played at blind side wing forward in Wales's last two teams of the previous season but was now picked to play for East Wales at No. 8. In the end Raybould had to withdraw because of shingles, but his place at centre was taken by another member of London Welsh, S. J. Dawes, who had already played eight times for his country since 1964.

Altogether the final East Wales team included seven Test players, three of whom had played for Wales against New Zealand a few weeks before. The three were W. K. Jones (there were three Joneses in the side) on the right wing and halfbacks Edwards (captain) and John. All three were from the Cardiff club. The other four were Dawes, R. Jones, O'Shea, a tough prop who had played against Scotland and Ireland the previous season, and T. G. R. (Gerald) Davies. Davies had come under the coaching of John Robins, the 1966 Lions' coach, at Loughborough and had since played in all Wales's five games in the 1966–67 season, gaining himself the reputation of being the best attacking centre in the British Isles. He had a leg injury at the time of the Wales-New Zealand game.

On paper, indeed, the East Wales backs looked a stronger combination than those who had represented Wales against New Zealand. The front row, too, was strong and hard, and the locks were tough and experienced. The wing forwards and No. 8 were all three aggressive players. The side had been chosen from a squad of 28 players named early in November and had been coached by Dai Hayward, the former Cardiff and Wales wing forward. The clash was eagerly awaited in Cardiff.

Unfortunately Cardiff came in for a sudden severe spell of cold weather. Although the paddock was covered by eight tons of straw as well as by tarpaulins, the game had to be postponed. The turf itself was found to be fit for play under the straw, but nearly a foot of snow had fallen, and the terraces were in no state to take the anticipated multitude. The snow, the tarpaulins, and the straw could have been cleared from the paddock in time to play the match. But since the Cardiff Labour Exchange was closed on the Saturday morning, the extra labour needed to clear the terraces was not available. The All Blacks had arranged to spend the whole of the following week in London in preparation for their match against the Barbarians at Twickenham. But they now agreed to make a train journey from London to Cardiff and back again on the Wednesday to play the match against East Wales. This of course meant that this game would be even more closely overshadowed by the Barbarians match, now to be played only three days later.

In the meantime, the All Blacks went to Twickenham on the Tuesday to see the University Match in which Cambridge beat Oxford by a try and a penalty goal to nothing. The Oxford side included two New Zealanders, both at prop forward. These were J. S. Baird, of Christ's College, Christchurch, Otago, and Canterbury, and P. A. Painter, of Hastings Boys' High School. T. P. Bedford, a South African Test player who had toured New Zealand with the 1965 Springboks, was at wing forward for Oxford, and O. C. Waldron, who had played twice for Ireland in 1966, was one of Oxford's locks. Yet the Cambridge forwards got well on top, and it was generally agreed that Cambridge would have won by a much more convincing margin had they not been geared to play negative Rugby. Chris Laidlaw must have wondered how he would fit into this type of Rugby during his stay at Oxford the following season. Certainly it seemed that Oxford could do with his presence and his influence. It was a pleasing thought that perhaps the outlook of Charlie Saxton would be passed to Oxford Rugby through Laidlaw.

MATCH FOURTEEN

v. EAST WALES
AT CARDIFF
WEDNESDAY, DECEMBER 13, 1967

East Wales

D. *Griffiths (Bridgend and Cardiff T.C.)*

W. K. *Jones (Cardiff)*, T. G. R. *Davies (Cardiff)*,
S. J. *Dawes (London Welsh)*, F. *Wilson (Cardiff)*

B. *John (Cardiff)*, G. *Edwards (Cardiff)*, capt.

R. *Jones (Coventry)*, A. I. *Gray (London Welsh)*,
I. C. *Jones (London Welsh)*, L. *Baxter (Cardiff)*,
J. *Hickey (Cardiff)*, B. *James (Bridgend)*, J.
Young (Harrogate), J. P. *O'Shea (Cardiff)*

All Blacks

W. F. *McCormick*

G. S. *Thorne*, W. L. *Davis*, A. G. *Steel*

G. F. *Kember*, M. A. *Herewini*

C. R. *Laidlaw*

B. J. *Lochore, capt.*, G. C. *Williams*, S. C.
Strahan, A. E. *Smith*, I. A. *Kirkpatrick*, K. F.
Gray, J. *Major*, E. J. *Hazlett*

REFEREE: F. B. LOVIS (England)

EAST WALES 3 POINTS

Try—Wilson

ALL BLACKS 3 POINTS

Try—Steel

Attacking the Attackers

CARDIFF ARMS PARK had lost its snow by Wednesday, December 13, but the turf was soft and slimy. A crowd of about 35,000 turned out to witness this check in the All Blacks' winning progress in a game which, for a long time, the Welshmen seemed bound to win. Looking back, it is easy to see that the All Blacks were psychologically vulnerable this day. For them, the big match of the week was the one against the Barbarians three days later. It was on Twickenham that their sights, however involuntarily, would be trained. Then there was the disturbance of having to leave a week in London and to travel to Cardiff on the morning of the match. Against this, the East Wales side were at a psychological peak, having waited eagerly to prove that they could do better than West Wales and Monmouthshire had done. With eight members of Cardiff in their ranks, they also possessed something of the high tradition of that club's great matches against touring teams.

On more material grounds, too, the All Blacks were vulnerable. They had their two rawest locks paired for only the second time of the tour. Herewini had not played for three weeks because of injury. And Herewini and Kember had not previously played together at five-eighth. Thorne was out of position on the right wing. The most important factor, however, was that East Wales were a good side, and that they played hard, imaginative, attacking Rugby.

The match had an especially boisterous start, involving several penalties, but both sides soon settled down to try to play constructive Rugby. The Welsh tried to follow the example of Scotland by reducing the number of players at line-outs. But this time the All Blacks were prepared, and the well-timed jumping of the tall Lochore and Kirkpatrick could frustrate the Welshmen in this ploy. Generally, however, it was the All Blacks who were frustrated in these early stages of the game. Herewini was not taking Laidlaw's passes safely, and so was giving the Welsh loose forwards early opportunities to make their presence felt as they hacked the ball on at their feet. In contrast to Herewini's troubles, Edwards and John soon began to combine with a fluency and dexterity which were to be one of the most potent features of the match.

The All Blacks' handling errors and the Welsh attacks meant that the New Zealanders were pinned in their own half. Once only a grand tackle by McCormick kept out Wilson after John had sold two dummies and sent Davies away. Then, after 22 minutes, came the Welsh try. Baxter tapped the ball down from a line-out, John let fly a dropkick which missed the target, and Wilson beat Thorne and McCormick to touch the ball down over the All Blacks' line.

As usual the All Blacks played some particularly strong Rugby immediately after their opponents had scored. The forwards made two or three powerful drives in which Gray and Hazlett were prominent, and there were some up-and-under kicks by Laidlaw. Steel once was not far from a try after a grubkick by Davis. But the Welsh too were still going strongly and worrying the All Blacks with their clever running and their astute kicking. Wilson was given two more runs and Griffiths took a penalty kick at goal. Half-time arrived with the score still 3–0 to the Welsh.

It was difficult to see how the All Blacks were going to escape. They were making far more mistakes than the Welsh, their own kicks were being brilliantly covered and fielded by John and Edwards, they were not as quick as the lighter Welsh in turning and recovering on the soft turf. And, though Laidlaw was standing up manfully to the pressure upon him, Herewini was right out of touch. The Welsh were deliberately kicking or passing the ball into the open spaces so as to avoid the close forward combat in which the New Zealanders' advantage in weight might have made itself felt. In maintaining this open play the Welsh were also making the best use of the mutual understanding of Edwards and John, the great attacking skill of Davies in the centre, and the pace of Keri

Jones and Wilson on the wings. The Welsh forwards, too, were playing with fine determination and were managing to a large extent to prevent the All Blacks from getting regular clean and quick possession from the rucks. Unless the All Blacks could transform themselves, they were in for a hard time in the second half.

And so it proved. In particular the All Blacks had three narrow escapes. First John kicked diagonally to the right, and Keri Jones and McCormick clashed in chasing the ball. The noisy crowd was sure East Wales would be given a penalty try for obstruction; but the referee decided that McCormick's was a fair shoulder charge. Next, Edwards dribbled the ball into the All Blacks' 25, and Wilson touched down for what the crowd thought was a try—but he had got the ball in an offside position. Then Edwards sold a dummy behind a scrum and caught Williams offside, but Edwards himself was just wide with the penalty kick at goal. Altogether Edwards and Griffiths failed with four penalty kicks at goal between them. Play was taking the same pattern and the same course as in the first half. The All Blacks were almost constantly under pressure.

It was from a position not far from their own line that the All Blacks began the move which ended in their try little more than ten minutes from time. A forward rush, in which Hazlett was prominent, took play up to halfway. Then there was a ruck from which Lochore passed the ball out left to the blind side. When Steel started his run, he had about 40 yards to go and there were defenders in the way. But Steel ran strongly as well as fast: breaking through two attempted tackles, he beat Keri Jones, Davies, and Griffiths for a try in the left corner. The crowd made a lot of noise while McCormick was attempting the crucial conversion, and the kick failed narrowly.

Could the All Blacks now bring off a grandstand finish such as they had at Newport, Bayonne, and Swansea? Not this time. They tried hard enough, but at the last it was the Welsh who were doing all the pressing. In the final seconds John, who had amply confirmed his promise and his versatility, was only just wide with a dropkick at goal. Fred Allen said the

All Blacks were lucky to get away with it. And Saxton said they would not have been worried by a beating from such a side.

Dai Hayward, the coach of the East Wales team, said he had decided that the only way to attempt to beat the All Blacks was to attack them. To a New Zealander, such a remark will sound naïve. But, coming from someone in a Britain too long stifled by defensive theories and a negative outlook, this was a remark of great significance. The All Blacks had taught throughout the tour that attacking football pays. East Wales had now shown, like the French, that the way to deal with an attacking side is to play attacking football yourself. This of course is an elementary point. But one of the most impressive features of the tour was that it went on and on emphasising and re-emphasising the simple truths of the sport.

Riches of Experience

AND SO BACK to London and to Twickenham for the great finale against the Barbarians. Where there was any room for doubt as to which of two players was really the best for his position at this stage of the tour, the All Blacks' selectors chose the senior player, the one who had given the longer service to New Zealand, the one who perhaps would never see Twickenham again. It was therefore a side rich in experience, a mellow team, that the All Blacks fielded for their last match.

McCormick, at full back, needed two points to reach his hundredth in Europe. Dick, on the right wing, had not played since Melrose and was still not 100 per cent fit. Davis was in the centre and Steel on the left wing. McRae, who had not played since the Scotland Test because of back trouble, was included at second five-eighth. Kirton returned at first five-eighth with Laidlaw at halfback.

The front row read Gray, McLeod, and Muller. At lock, Meads returned after suspension to play his 99th game in the All Black jersey. Strahan, inevitably at this stage of the tour, was to be his partner at lock, and Nathan and Tremain were preferred to Williams and Kirkpatrick on the flanks. It was good that Nathan, whose jaw injury had meant his missing all the four Tests, should be given a place in this final team. Lochore, who had played one game at lock and all the rest at No. 8, had missed only two matches, those at Swansea, where Meads captained the side, and at Bayonne, where MacRae was captain. This therefore was Lochore's thirteenth game. This was two more than anyone else, the nearest being McCormick and Davis each with eleven appearances.

Because of the risk of carrying foot-and-mouth disease, which had so far been kept out of Ireland, no Irish players were included in the Barbarians' fifteen. Apart from the regrettable absence of the Irish, the team was not far from the strongest that could be raised from the British Isles on current form. The players would be conscious that they had here a chance to make a name for themselves with a view towards selection for the Lions' party due to tour South Africa in 1968.

As originally chosen, the Barbarians' team included only three players who had been on the 1966 Lions' tour of New Zealand. These were Stewart Wilson at full-back, Frank Laidlaw at hooker, and Howard Norris at loose head prop. But Pringle Fisher, Scotland's captain, had to withdraw with hamstring trouble, and his place at wing forward was taken by Derrick Grant, of the 1966 Lions. The only one of the fifteen who had not already played against the All Blacks on this tour was Norris, who had been eligible for East Wales and for Wales but had not won favour. Keri Jones on the right wing and Gareth Edwards and Barry John at halfback had already played twice against the All Blacks, for Wales and for East Wales, the latter game having been only three days before this Barbarians' match. Gerald Davies had also played against the All Blacks on the previous Wednesday. The six English-men in the side had also already played twice against the New Zealanders.

There was every reason to expect an attacking game of exciting football. On the All Blacks' previous visit to Twicken-ham they had played their highest quality football of the tour—the best balanced Rugby most of us had ever seen—in the first 45 minutes against England. The last meeting between the Barbarians and All Blacks, the final game of the 1963–64 tour, had produced a great game won by the New Zealanders by 36-3 at Cardiff, the last of eight tries being scored by Wilson Whineray, New Zealand's captain and predecessor of Brian Lochore. The Saturday morning now was fine and sunny, the snows of the previous weekend had vanished, and Twickenham's drains had done their work well.

MATCH FIFTEEN

v. BARBARIANS
AT TWICKENHAM
SATURDAY, DECEMBER 16, 1967

Barbarians

S. Wilson (Scotland), capt.

W. K. Jones (Wales), T. G. R. Davies (Wales), R. H. Lloyd (England), R. E. Webb (England)

B. John (Wales), G. Edwards (Wales)

G. A. Sheriff (England), R. B. Taylor (England), P. J. Larter (England), M. Wiltshire (Wales), D. Grant (Scotland), C. H. Norris (Wales), F. A. L. Laidlaw (Scotland), A. L. Horton (England)

All Blacks

W. F. McCormick

M. J. Dick, W. L. Davis, A. G. Steel

I. R. MacRae, E. W. Kirton

C. R. Laidlaw

B. J. Lochore, capt., W. J. Nathan, S. C. Strahan, C. E. Meads, K. R. Tremain, K. F. Gray, B. E. McLeod, B. L. Muller

REFEREE: M. JOSEPH *(Wales)*

BARBARIANS 6 POINTS

Try—Lloyd; dropped goal—Wilson

ALL BLACKS 11 POINTS

2 tries—MacRae, Steel; dropped goal—Kirton; conversion—McCormick

A Wonderful Finish

BECAUSE OF THE tall stands, with gaps between them in the North-East and North-West corners, Twickenham is an awkward ground for wind. The Barbarians won the toss and decided to have a northerly breeze behind them. There was a crowd of about 40,000 to see the Barbarians make an early challenge. Wiltshire intercepted Dick's throw-in to the first line-out, and a high kick to the right by John led to McCormick's being swamped. Lochore put in a riposte for New Zealand by getting the ball back from a long throw-in by Webb, but Chris Laidlaw's subsequent relieving kick just failed to reach the touchline—perhaps because of the tricky wind currents. Wilson cradled it gracefully, took very deliberate aim, and released a perfectly struck dropkick which sailed unerringly between the posts.

This was after four minutes' play—and, as usual after a score by their opponents, the All Blacks reacted strongly. Meads peeled from the back of a line-out and other forwards carried on. McCormick came into the line, ran through, and passed inside. A Barbarian heel from a set scrum was wrecked by a powerful controlled wheel by the All Blacks. The New Zealanders hooked the ball against the head. Kirton ran across in front of MacRae and passed the ball inside to him. Then Strahan pulled the ball down from a great height at a line-out on the left, and Kirton dropped a skilful goal through the eddies of wind coming between the North and West stands. After eleven minutes it was 3-3.

After a while we had Lochore decoying the defence towards the blind side while Laidlaw sent the ball instead to Kirton on the open side. But then we saw the first signs of frailty in the All Blacks' backs. Davis dropped the ball in a line movement, and Grant was away with it in a flash. Then McCormick, under pressure, failed to put a clearance kick over the touchline, an All Black got offside in chasing it, and Wilson hit a post high up with the long and difficult penalty kick.

A firm tackle by Lloyd prevented MacRae from breaking. When MacRae next did break inside Lloyd a tenacious smother stopped him from feeding the ball to his supporting pack. A grubkick by Kirton for Steel looked more promising, but the All Blacks gave away a penalty at a maul: they did not retire 10 yards when the Barbarians took a tap, and Wilson's second penalty kick at goal only just missed its target. Lochore sought to impose authority and stability by checking a set heel and trundling the Barbarians backwards, but Laidlaw's kick from behind this scrum was charged down. Steel came into the line at Kirton's elbow and tore through, but the All Blacks were again penalised, this time at a set scrum. This kick, however, was from inside the Barbarians' half, and Wilson was both wide and short.

The Barbarians were scarcely getting any possession from the set pieces and consequently were doing very little attacking. Yet it was they who were having the chances to kick goals because the All Blacks' backs were making so many mistakes. For a moment the All Blacks showed us one of the old-time tricks, Gray pulling the ball down near the front of a line-out for Tremain to force his way through close to the touchline. But then the Barbarians did manage to launch an attack—by bypassing the difficulties. Jones on the right threw the ball in long over the top of the line-out direct to John, and the ball was passed all along the line to Webb on the left. It was notable, however, that when Webb was tackled it was not a Barbarian but Nathan who made off with the loose ball. And at last, after 32 minutes' play, McCormick had his first penalty kick at goal, the Barbarians having offended at a set scrum. The kick missed.

In the few minutes left before halftime there were two unusual lapses from Kirton. First he dropped the ball in trying to come into a move a second time, and then he sliced a kick-ahead so badly that Webb was given a run for the Barbarians. Kirton made up for one of these errors with a fine piece of covering after the Barbarians' Davies had kicked ahead and caught his own kick. But when MacRae called the All Blacks'

Davis for a scissors, Davis dropped the ball. The Barbarians finished the half strongly. They tapped the ball down to Norris at the back of a line-out, and John sent a diagonal kick dangerously to the right. From a set scrum on the left John sent a dropkick just under the bar. And, after a large All Black hand had been seen getting the ball from a loose scrum, Wilson, with his fourth penalty kick at goal, hit a post for the second time. So it was still 3-3 at the interval.

The All Blacks' forwards had won enough of the ball for their side to have been well ahead by this stage, but the handling of the backs had been strangely inept. Had something gone wrong with Fred Allen's seemingly infallible coaching methods? The backs had not handled well at Cardiff or Newport in their two previous games. It was odd to remember how wonderfully well they had given and taken their passes on this same ground against England six weeks before when the ball had been wet and slippery. Now that it was dry, they were dropping it and even passing it on to the ground.

During the interval the Barbarians must have blessed their good fortune and gained in confidence. Afterwards they got more of the ball and were able to make some worthwhile attacks. They made use of Taylor at the back of the line-out, and shortly after the start of the second half Edwards took a quick dropkick at goal in the loose which missed. For the All Blacks, both Laidlaw and Kirton did rather more kicking than before, which was sensible in the circumstances, and MacRae for a while changed places with Davis. But when the All Blacks tried to get McCormick to make one of his dummy entries into the line, a feeble pass fell limply short of the man who was meant to receive it, and Kirton again knocked on.

The disease seemed to be catching. When John made a break on the blind side of a set scrum, Webb knocked on. Less than a minute later John himself knocked on. In no time the All Blacks had cleared their lines, and at last they achieved two promising movements, in each case Laidlaw passing to the right direct to Davis who was now at second five-eighth. In the first, Steel came into the line outside MacRae: in the second McCormick came in also outside MacRae. In addition a high kick to the left by Kirton put

Wilson under pressure. The All Blacks' backs seemed to be recovering their confidence.

But they still had torments to suffer. Another dropped pass led to a long and fast run by Keri Jones on the right. McCormick showed his defensive positional skill as a full-back by shepherding Jones towards the touchline. But when Jones kicked the ball over McCormick's head, probably only a superb piece of covering by Davis, who raced back, prevented a try. Then John made another break and kicked ahead, the Barbarians won the maul, John kicked through again, and Lloyd touched down for a try. It was his fourth try in three games against the All Blacks. He scored one in the game at Leicester and two for England. He remained the only Englishman to score a try against the 1967 All Blacks.

So, after 18 minutes of the second half, the Barbarians led 6-0, Wilson having narrowly failed with the difficult conversion kick. Those of us who had followed the All Blacks from match to match felt that now was the moment the New Zealanders would make their supreme effort and would sweep to victory. They made the effort all right and were soon attacking hard at the other end. After a tremendous rush Nathan almost got over. Then there was a set scrum a few feet from the Barbarians' line with the All Blacks to put in. Lochore detached himself and stood out of it, and we watched intently to see which of his variations would bring the try. But Horton knows a thing or two about tight head propping, Laidlaw is a good hooker, and the Barbarians' pack were nothing if not dogged and determined. The ball came out on the Barbarians' side.

The All Blacks' assault was not yet spent, and soon Laidlaw got the ball from a maul following a line-out, and his dropkick flew just outside the right hand post. Then the Barbarians were caught offside at the back of a line-out, and the All Blacks decided to run the ball from a tapped penalty; but Davis hesitated and lost the ball in a tackle.

Now it was the Barbarians' turn to attack, and John sent a raking diagonal kick to the right. The Barbarians heeled against the head, and John kicked naggingly through. The All Blacks were being frustrated right and left and, horror of horrors, Strahan was penalised for coming into the wrong side of a maul. The kick, about halfway out on the right, was not a difficult one for Wilson. Thirty minutes of the second half had gone, and a Barbarians lead of 9-3 would have meant that the All Blacks would have to score twice in ten minutes plus injury time. These are the moments when you think of the splendour of those moves against England, the brilliant light and colour of Toulouse, the blood and thunder of Colombes. Why wouldn't it come right for the All Blacks now when they wanted it so badly? Thoughts were cut short: Wilson's kick was not going over. It missed.

Back came the All Blacks, and this time they caught Wilson in possession behind his own line after a pass by Edwards—another set scrum with New Zealand to put in. This time the All Blacks did hook the ball, but they heeled it so strongly that it went straight out of the scrum direct to Kirton at first five-eighth. He did the only thing possible: he put his head down and went for the line. But the Barbarians got hold of him, and in no time the ball was in the hands of Davies, who was streaking away upfield to the right. Somehow McCormick got across and outmanoeuvred Davies as he had Jones earlier, and now the ball was being borne swiftly and menacingly back by Nathan—now Tremain was charging for the line with it.

This was wonderful stuff. The crowd was in uproar, and even Meads was inspired to jump high at a line-out. From his jump Kirton tried to come into the line a second time as he had so perfectly at Murrayfield and at Newport; but the Barbarians were ready for him. Then, when one minute of ordinary time was left, the All Blacks took a tapped penalty in their own half on the right. Out came the ball towards the left, and McCormick joined in. The Barbarians managed to check the move but not to stifle it, and in a trice the All Blacks had switched the ball back towards the right and Steel had come tearing through in the middle. Steel ran straight at the last defender, bumped into him, and although off balance, managed to send the ball in the direction of MacRae outside him who scored.

So the match hung on McCormick's kick which, like Wilson's just ten minutes before it, was not really a very difficult one. But Twickenham, like most of the grounds on which the All Blacks played, made a din while he was kicking, and the ball went wide. The crowd settled for a draw.

But the All Blacks were not settling for a draw. They ran the ball out from their own 25, and Kirton kicked diagonally. Then, after three minutes of injury time, Laidlaw seemed to have wasted a chance by kicking the ball straight to Wilson. But Wilson's punt did not reach touch and Lochore, as ever, was in position to field it. Lochore instantly saw the chance and headed for the Barbarians' line. Kirton went with him, took his pass, and veered slightly inwards, keeping the defence away from the left touchline. Just when he was wanted, Steel came steaming up at speed for the scoring pass and the winning try.

McCormick's conversion was of academic interest only, but it brought him his hundredth point in Europe. All that was left now was *Now is the Hour*, *Auld Lang Syne*, the carrying of Lochore and for a little while Meads, shoulder high, and a host of wonderful memories.

Match Details

MATCH NUMBER	SCORES AND SCORERS
1	**NORTH OF ENGLAND 3 POINTS** Penalty goal—Chapman **ALL BLACKS 33 POINTS** 6 tries—Birtwistle (2), Williams (2), Going, McCormick; 3 conversions—McCormick; 3 penalty goals—McCormick
2	**MIDLANDS, LONDON AND HOME COUNTIES 3 POINTS** Try—Lloyd **ALL BLACKS 15 POINTS** Try—Dick; dropped goal—Herewini; 3 penalty goals—McCormick
3	**SOUTH OF ENGLAND 3 POINTS** Penalty goal—Rutherford **ALL BLACKS 16 POINTS** 4 tries—Steel, Kirton, Going, Birtwistle; 2 conversions—Kember
4	**ENGLAND 11 POINTS** 2 tries—Lloyd (2); conversion—Rutherford; penalty goal—Larter **NEW ZEALAND 23 POINTS** 5 tries—Kirton (2), Birtwistle, Laidlaw, Dick; 4 conversions—McCormick

Match Details—CONTINUED

MATCH NUMBER	SCORES AND SCORERS
5	**WEST WALES 14 POINTS** Try—H. Williams; 3 penalty goals—D. Rees; conversion—D. Rees **ALL BLACKS 21 POINTS** 4 tries—Thorne (2), Meads, Going; 3 conversions—Kember; penalty goal—Kember
6	**WALES 6 POINTS** Dropped goal—John; penalty goal—Gale **NEW ZEALAND 13 POINTS** 2 tries—Birtwistle, Davis; 2 conversions—McCormick; penalty goal—McCormick
7	**SOUTH-EAST FRANCE 3 POINTS** Dropped goal—G. Camberabero **ALL BLACKS 16 POINTS** 4 tries—McLeod, Steel (2), Kirkpatrick; 2 conversions—Kember
8	**FRANCE B 19 POINTS** 2 tries—Plantefol, Lux; 3 penalty goals—Villepreux; 2 conversions—Villepreux **ALL BLACKS 32 POINTS** 5 tries—Williams (2), Dick, Going, Kirkpatrick; dropped goal—Cottrell; 4 conversions—McCormick; 2 penalty goals—McCormick

Match Details—CONTINUED

MATCH NUMBER	SCORES AND SCORERS
9	**SOUTH-WEST FRANCE 14 POINTS** Try—Latanne; 3 penalty goals—Dehez; conversion—Dehez **ALL BLACKS 18 POINTS** 3 tries—Kirkpatrick, Dick, Tremain; 3 penalty goals—Kember
10	**FRANCE 15 POINTS** Try—Campaes; dropped goal—Gachassin; 3 penalty goals—Villepreux **NEW ZEALAND 21 POINTS** 4 tries—Going, Steel, Kirkpatrick, Dick; 3 conversions—McCormick; penalty goal—McCormick
11	**SCOTTISH DISTRICTS 14 POINTS** Try—Gill; conversion—Blaikie; 3 penalty goals—Blaikie **ALL BLACKS 35 POINTS** 7 tries—Birtwistle (3), Thorne, Laidlaw, Hopkinson, Nathan; 4 conversions—McCormick; 2 penalty goals—McCormick
12	**SCOTLAND 3 POINTS** dropped goal—Chisholm **NEW ZEALAND 14 POINTS** 2 tries—MacRae, Davis; conversion—McCormick; 2 penalty goals—McCormick

Match Details—CONTINUED

MATCH NUMBER	SCORES AND SCORERS
13	**MONMOUTHSHIRE 12 POINTS** 4 penalty goals—Jarrett **ALL BLACKS 23 POINTS** 4 tries—Kirton, Steel, Tremain, Muller; conversion—McCormick; 3 penalty goals—McCormick
14	**EAST WALES 3 POINTS** Try—Wilson **ALL BLACKS 3 POINTS** Try—Steel
15	**BARBARIANS 6 POINTS** Try—Lloyd; dropped goal—Wilson **ALL BLACKS 11 POINTS** 2 tries—MacRae, Steel; dropped goal—Kirton; conversion—McCormick

Table of Scorers

Player	No. of matches	Tries	Conversions	Penalty goals	Dropped goals	Points
W. F. McCormick	11	1	23	17	—	100
G. F. Kember	6	—	7	4	—	26
W. M. Birtwistle	7	8	—	—	—	24
A. G. Steel	10	7	—	—	—	21
E. W. Kirton	9	4	—	—	1	15
M. J. Dick	8	5	—	—	—	15
S. M. Going	7	5	—	—	—	15
G. C. Williams	8	4	—	—	—	12
I. A. Kirkpatrick	7	4	—	—	—	12
G. S. Thorne	6	3	—	—	—	9
W. L. Davis	11	2	—	—	—	6
K. R. Tremain	9	2	—	—	—	6
C. R. Laidlaw	8	2	—	—	—	6
I. R. MacRae	7	2	—	—	—	6
C. E. Meads	10	1	—	—	—	3
B. E. McLeod	9	1	—	—	—	3
B. L. Muller	8	1	—	—	—	3
A. E. Hopkinson	7	1	—	—	—	3
W. D. Cottrell	7	—	—	—	1	3
M. A. Herewini	5	—	—	—	1	3
W. J. Nathan	5	1	—	—	—	3
B. J. Lochore	13	—	—	—	—	—
S. C. Strahan	10	—	—	—	—	—
K. F. Gray	9	—	—	—	—	—
E. J. Hazlett	6	—	—	—	—	—
J. Major	6	—	—	—	—	—
A. G. Jennings	5	—	—	—	—	—
A. E. Smith	4	—	—	—	—	—
M. C. Wills	4	—	—	—	—	—
P. H. Clarke	3	—	—	—	—	—

Points Analysis

FULL RECORD

Played: 15. Won: 14. Drawn: 1.
Points for: 294. Points against: 129.

TEST RECORD

Played: 4. Won: 4. Points for: 71. Points against: 35.

LEADING SCORERS

McCormick: 100 points. Kember: 26 points. Birtwistle: 24 points. Steel: 21 points.

MOST APPEARANCES

Lochore: 13. Davis: 11. McCormick: 11. Meads: 10. Steel: 10. Strahan: 10.

POINTS

The All Blacks' 294 points came from 54 tries, 30 conversions, 21 penalty goals, 3 dropped goals.

Their opponents' 129 points came from 11 tries, 6 conversions, 23 penalty goals, 5 dropped goals.

TRIES

The 1967 All Blacks scored 54 tries in 15 matches and converted 30 (more than half of total).

The 1963-64 All Blacks scored 111 tries in 34 matches and converted 47 (fewer than half of total).

PENALTY GOALS

The 1967 All Blacks scored 63 of their 294 points from penalty goals.

Their opponents scored 69 of their 129 points from penalty goals.

Total weight of the All Blacks' thirty players was 2 tons, 12 cwts, 50 lbs. Roughly half of this weight—1 ton, 6 cwts, 25 lbs—would therefore be on the field for any given match.